To Cindy + Steven

May It =
Bless you.

Shalom

John David

ORDAINED
TO BE A JEW

ORDAINED TO BE A JEW

A Catholic Priest's Conversion to Judaism

John David Scalamonti

KTAV PUBLISHING HOUSE, INC.
HOBOKEN, NJ

Library of Congress Cataloging-in-Publication Data

Scalamonti, John David,
    Ordained to be a Jew : a Catholic priest's conversion to Judaism.
        p.   cm.
    ISBN 0-88125-412-6
    1. Scalamonti, John David. 2. Proselytes and proselyting. Jewish-
-Converts from Christianity--Biography. 3. Jews--United States-
-Biography. 4. Ex-priests. Catholic--United States--Biography.
I. Title.
BM755.S249A3 1992
296.7'1--dc20   92-25994
                                                               CIP

Manufactured in the United States of America

Contents

Dedication

This book is dedicated to my mother-in-law, Gertrude Max, and to the loving memory of my father-in-law, Sidney Max. Without their example and love of Judaism, this story would not exist. Without their influence, I would have been deprived of the honor of being one of God's Chosen.

Acknowledgments

I wish to thank my wife, Diane, for her encouragement, her comments, and her valuable suggestions. She is a true help-mate, a loving wife, and a devoted mother. I thank God that I met her, for only He knows what would have become of me otherwise.

I also wish to thank Shelley Einhorn for her sincere interest and encouragement in the writing of this book. I am indebted to my publisher, Bernard Scharfstein, who gave me the opportunity to have my story published, and to my editor and friend, Yaakov Elman, whose counsel and direction contributed greatly to the refinement of this book.

Preface

When I set out to write this book, I naturally approached many publishers and experts in the field to see whether they thought the subject matter would be of interest to readers. Most felt it would be, but at the same time warned that an autobiographical book by an unknown named John David Scalamonti would not break any records. I couldn't have agreed with them more, but my purpose in writing this book was not to have people read about me. Although it is essential that I recount details about my life, I am writing not about myself but about a precious gift that was given me. A gift I want to share with others—and most especially with those who have been given the same gift at birth but do not sufficiently appreciate it. The gift of which I write is the faith of Abraham, Isaac, and Jacob. A faith now centuries old, but as new and living as on the day it was first given to Abraham. A faith I have come to know and love. A faith that truly reflects God's love for His creation and His people. It is the faith of Judaism.

My journey from the priesthood to the conversion rite of the *mikvah* reveals the circumstances and events which brought me to that moment in my life when God—and only He knows why—decided to give me this precious gift.

Boyhood Dreams

From the plane I could see the large columns of black slate and the scarred landscape left by those who had strip-mined this once beautiful land for coal. I was approaching Avoca Airport, which serviced the Scranton/Wilkes-Barre area in northeastern Pennsylvania. I was wearing my newly purchased black suit and Roman collar and feeling quite proud of what it represented. This was my first time traveling as an ordained priest, and it was a thrill to be called "father." With my ordination behind me I was coming back to the place where I had lived my boyhood and where my journey to the priesthood had its origin. I was coming home to celebrate my first public mass. I wondered if any of my grammar school classmates and boyhood friends would attend. It would be great to see them. Some I had not seen in many years. I closed my eyes and began to reminisce over my childhood, searching for the reason or reasons that had set me out on this journey.

I was the first-born of Elizabeth and Adam Scalamonti on January 18, 1941. I was baptized into the Roman Catholic faith and became a member of Saint Michael's Slovak Church in my hometown of Jessup. My mother's parents were of Slavic heritage, their roots stemming from Eastern Europe. My father's parents were both from Italy, my grandmother from Sicily and my grandfather from Naples. I shared a modest home with my parents, my mother's mother, and my three younger brothers, Michael, Andrew, and Charles. My sister, Maria, would later be born while I was attending the minor seminary.

My hometown of Jessup, which is located near Scranton, represents the kind of place where one would want to bring up one's children. The town is nestled between the mountains and sheltered from the many problems of our major cities and large suburbs. It boasted a population of about six thousand residents back in 1941 and still does; nothing changes. When Diane and I visit there with our children, we often remark about how behind the times the town appears to be.

Ethnically, Jessup is predominantly Irish, Italian, Polish, and Slovak. There are five Catholic churches and one Protestant church; at one time there was even a synagogue. When I was a boy, the town's Jewish population consisted of about five families. The Weisses owned and operated the five-and-ten. The Mandels owned the automotive-parts store (their son Howard was a close friend of my uncle Mike). Our shoes were always purchased from Mr. Strassman, who owned the shoe store. The Theirs family owned the clothing store, and groceries were often purchased from the Swagenbaums.

It seemed to me that the town was devoid of prejudice. Its residents respected each other, and I was not aware of any hostility toward the Jews who lived there. I can only recall feelings of sorrow for them, believing that even though they were nice people they would probably not go to heaven when they died. Aside from this we all respected them, for we knew that they were well educated and intelligent. My mother used to say to my brothers, "Find yourselves a rich Jewish girl to marry," never thinking that someday I would be married to one.

The prejudice I heard was always couched in positive terms, such as, "Jews are rich, they stick together," or "they take care of their own." That was the extent of any anti-

Semitism in my family. Our town's Jews were the only Jewish people I knew as a young boy. Later, as a priest, I always made a point of dropping in at their stores to say hello when I was home on vacation. All of them attended my first public mass and reception.

I don't remember my parents being very religious. They were members of the parish church and saw to it that my three brothers and I attended the parish school. We all made our first communions and confirmations. We attended mass on Sundays and other holy days and observed the laws of the church—no meat on Fridays and observing the Lenten season by fasting and giving up candy and the movies. Neither my mother nor my father ever suggested or in any way hinted that they would like to see one of their sons aspire to the priesthood. When the time came for me to reveal my dream of becoming a priest, my mother was the stumbling block.

I received my grammar school education at the parish school, known as Saint Michael's Parochial School. Everyone has heard stories about the strict discipline imposed on the students in Catholic schools by the nuns who are their teachers. I can confirm that the stories are all true. On a few occasions I had the palms of my hand hit with a ruler for throwing snowballs. Once, while only in the second grade and about seven years of age, I was made to sit on a chair near the oil burner in the convent's dark basement as punishment for not doing my math homework. I was absolutely petrified that the burner was going to blow up and I would be killed. I often blame that horrible experience for my deficiencies in math. I knew a girl in the sixth grade whose ear was injured by a clock thrown at her by one of the nuns. And in those days the parents always sided with the nuns, so there was no recourse. In all fairness, I suppose that most Catholics who attended parochial school graduated with a good education and a great respect for the word *discipline*.

While in second grade I had my first taste of the Latin

language. My goal at that age was to become an altar boy,
but first I had to master the Latin of the mass. I remember
how diligently I committed to memory the Latin phrases
and responses one had to know. I still remember the very
first prayer and response I learned as an altar boy: *Ad Deum
qui laetificat juventutem meam*, "to God who is the joy of my
youth." And so Christmas Eve of 1948 was going to be extra
exciting for me, or so I thought. Having passed the Latin test
and memorized the prayers, I was to serve as an altar boy at
the Midnight Mass.

But that same year I also discovered the unthinkable,
namely, that Santa Claus didn't exist. Since I would have to
stay up late on Christmas Eve, my parents had no choice but
to tell me the "facts" about Santa. My brothers had long
since gone to bed, anxious for morning to arrive. My father
motioned for me to sit next to him on our sofa. He then
began, what I am sure was very difficult for him, the unwel-
come task of telling me, in no uncertain terms, that there
really was no Santa Claus. Tears ran down my cheeks as my
dad's words took from me a Christmas fantasy that every
child has the right to enjoy. So it appeared that to gain the
privilege of being an altar boy I had to give up a special
fantasy. The aspect of sacrificing something secular in order
to gain a spiritual goal would become, in later years, a fact
of life for me.

I cannot pinpoint any special person, place, or experience
that led me in the direction of wanting to become a priest. I
enjoyed serving mass, and I know that I was very impressed
by its rituals, so much so that I often would play mass at
home. My grandparents had an old piano in their front
parlor, and when no one was home I would wrap towels
around my shoulders and waist which served as priestly
robes, stand before the piano, which served as the altar, and
pretend to say mass. I would cut circular segments from
some slices of bread that in imagination resembled the large,
round host used by the priest. Water would take the place of

the wine, and a dictionary or any large book would serve as the Scriptures from which I would pretend to read the Latin.

This "mass playing" continued until one day I forgot to discard the leftover pieces of bread with the holes in them where I had cut out the host-like circles. When my mother asked me about the bread I quickly confessed. My parents forgave me but admonished that I was not to waste bread since this was a sin. From then on, when playing mass, I had to resort to cutting out circles from white paper. They were fine until the time came to consume them.

I don't want to give the impression that I was abnormal or that I was some kind of angel. I did my fair share of childhood pranks both at home and in school. And as in many other families, I had a few fights with my brothers, and received my fair share of spankings. I attended birthday parties and played Post Office and Spin the Bottle, games that gave the boys a chance to kiss a girl without being teased by their peers. I even, while in the seventh grade, went to a movie with a girl from my class. I especially enjoyed listening to my favorite radio shows, such as "The Lone Ranger," "The Green Hornet," and "Sky King." The next day, with my brothers and playmates, I would act out the radio adventures that had so stimulated our imaginations.

In general, I enjoyed a normal childhood and did what the other kids my age did. As I grew older, however, the desire to become a priest only strengthened. I would still play mass, now employing the services of my younger brothers as my altar boys. Many times they would complain about this forced religious practice, but my being the oldest and the strongest ensured their cooperation.

I grew up during the late forties and early fifties. It was a wonderful time for everyone. I was old enough to remember my father and uncles coming home from the war. I remember President Truman and then the fatherly President Eisenhower. Life seemed so much simpler then. The values of honesty, respect for authority, and common decency seemed to be shared by all. People didn't question authority, civil or religious, at least not openly. My home represented the values of family, honesty, responsibility, and work.

My father's work often took him out of town for months. He was a musician at that time, and the engagements of his band took him to states as far south as Virginia and as far west as Illinois. My mother worked in a shoe factory in a neighboring town. The responsibility of getting myself and my brothers off to school with breakfast in our stomachs fell upon my grandmother, who lived with us. She was like a second mother. But even with her help I often found myself fulfilling the role of helpmate to my mother. When my baby brother woke up during the night, I would go down to the kitchen to heat his formula and put him back to sleep, thus allowing my mother to get her needed rest. I took jobs delivering papers to help as much as I could with the strained finances of the household. It seemed that we never had enough money.

Outside the house my life was involved with Boy Scout meetings and other social activities. I joined the American Legion drum and bugle corps, in which I played the bass bugle. I would have preferred the drums, but you took whatever they gave you. I participated in the annual parades and enjoyed the friendships found there. Little League baseball filled the spring months with activity, and evenings were often spent practicing on the accordion, which I enjoyed and for which I seemed to have a talent.

I guess my musical talent came from my dad, as he was always quick to point out. Later, when I decided to enter the seminary I discovered to my disappointment that I would have to discontinue my lessons. I know my dad was upset about this. I think he always wanted one of us to follow in his footsteps and someday join his band. My musical talents were not altogether wasted, though. In the major seminary, I became director of the seminary choir, a role which I very much enjoyed.

When I began the eighth grade, the idea of possibly going on to a minor seminary at the end of the year intensified all the more my now clear desire to become a priest. I informed my parents of my intentions, and believe me, they were not happy.

My father's reaction was almost predictable: "I thought you wanted to play the accordion and someday be a musician. If this is what you want to do, okay, but it's really up to your mother."

My mother was adamantly opposed to my plan. "You're too young to leave home and to know what you want to be. Studying to be a priest is a very hard road. Go to a regular high school and college first, then if you still think you want to be a priest you can go to the seminary."

Maybe mom felt herself unworthy to have a son a priest, or maybe she feared that I would drop out and would return home a failure. We both knew of other fellows from our small town who had entered seminaries to become priests only to return home in disgrace for not having made it. Leaving the seminary in those days brought a definite social stigma upon the seminarian and his family. Neighbors and friends would whisper about it, offering opinions as to why the young man had not remained in the seminary. Had he left on his own or was he expelled? Was there a girl involved? Maybe he wasn't intelligent enough. And so went the gossip and opinions.

On the other hand, having a son in the seminary bestowed on the family a new, elevated social status in the church and community. It was almost as good as saying that you had a son studying to be a doctor or a dentist. So why my mother was so opposed to the idea of my entering the seminary I'll never know. I did know, however, that it was going to be very difficult to win her over. My persistence forced her to accept the fact that I was serious about becoming a priest, but nothing was going to make her allow me to enter the minor seminary at the end of the year. She insisted that I attend high school and college, and promised that if I still wanted the priesthood at that point she would support my decision.

Her attitude was very disappointing. The idea of waiting till I completed college before entering the seminary was not what I hoped to hear. I had already told most of my classmates and the nuns in school that I would be entering a seminary in the fall. Now I had to tell them that I wouldn't be going away. I certainly did not want to attend the public high school, so I decided to enroll in St. Patrick's High School in a neighboring town. Since my parents did not have the money for my tuition, I discussed my financial problem with the principal. She agreed to waive the tuition if I would stay after school three days a week to clean some of the classrooms.

And so I began my first year of high school at St. Patrick's. When I told Sister Jeromine, my homeroom teacher, about my strong desire to enter a seminary, she gave me the names of some priests who at one time had been students of hers, suggesting that I write and tell them.

The priests she recommended were members of a religious community called the Missionaries of Our Lady of La Salette. The La Salette Fathers as they are generally known, operated a minor seminary in Hartford, Connecticut, and candidates for the priesthood were accepted at all grade levels. That meant that I could enter the seminary the following September as a sophomore.

With this information in hand, it didn't take me long to get a letter off to the director of vocations, Father James Hurley. In the letter I told him how I wanted to be a priest and would like to enter the seminary in the fall. I also said that my mother did not approve of this idea and didn't seem to want me to become a priest. I sent the letter in the hope that he would soon respond with some advice.

Weeks went by and no letter came for me. Terribly disappointed but not ready to give up on my dream, I began to inquire about other high school seminaries. One day, when I arrived home from school, my mother met me at the kitchen door. She looked upset and a bit angry. "John, go into the parlor." I walked past her into the room, and there, sitting on our sofa, were two priests.

"Hi John, I'm Father James Hurley, and this is Father Jim Jacobson." I was thrilled. They were attending a vocation conference in Scranton for the next few days and, since they were in the area, had made a special effort to find our home in order to meet with me and my parents. They had brought my letter along, and my mother had read it before I came home. I guess that was why she seemed so upset and angry.

After the introductions the priests didn't wait long before telling my mother how wrong it would be for her to stop me from entering the seminary at an early age. "A call to be a priest came from God," they said. "When a young man responded to that call, he had to be placed where the seed of his vocation could be protected from the evil elements of the world. A young vocation, being so tender, needed to be nurtured so that it would grow to fruition."

That sounded good to me! I could see my mother's face begin to betray confusion. She was always so sure of herself. They were obviously getting to her, especially when they emphasized that if she kept me home and sent me to a regular high school and college, the chances that I would lose my vocation would increase. If that were to happen, she would be accountable to God for a lost vocation, the church would lose a future priest, and the hundreds of souls I would have saved might lose their souls to the devil. And they had stories to back up their words.

Well, that did it! Talk about making a person feel guilty! She could no longer resist the two priests and their "holy" arguments.

"But wait," she said. "we are a poor family, we'd never be able to afford the tuition."

Father Hurley answered, "Mrs. Scalamonti, we would

never allow financial problems to stand in the way of what appears to be a true vocation. We have a program at the seminary for just such a situation as yours, and you are not the only one. The program is sponsored by wealthy benefactors of the seminary. They adopt a seminarian, I mean it's a spiritual adoption, they pay the seminarian's tuition. You don't have to worry about the money."

That did it! I felt sorry for my mother, but at the same time I was happy they had won. She turned to me and asked, "Is this what you really want to do?" I answered, "Yes, mom, I want this more than anything else in the world. Please can I go?"

"Go," she said, "I guess I can't stop you now, but you'd better stay with it."

I remember kissing her and promising that she wouldn't be sorry. The two priests left, confident that they had secured another recruit for the September enrollment. For me the preparations would soon begin for a journey that would take twelve years to complete. My mother was preparing herself for a painful separation from her fourteen-year-old son.

The Beginning of My Journey

I had, as a young boy, never been away from home and parents, with the sole exception of a two-week Boy Scout camping trip. I was a good son to my parents, especially to my mother. I tried to help her in every way that a boy my age could help. My father wasn't home very much while I was growing up. His career in music kept him out of town most of the year. He was and is a good father and had to do what was best to support us. I, being the oldest of the three at that time, filled in where I could as the man of the house. So when we started out that September day for the seminary, the sorrow in my mother's heart was visible through the tears she shed. For me it was the first step on a journey that I had been longing to take. For her it was the beginning of a long period of separation from her son. What added to the sorrow was that neither of us knew for certain whether the journey would end at its destination.

Since my father was out of town at the time, my mother had to drive the whole distance. One of her sisters, my aunt Clara, came with us to keep her company on the return trip. Although I was certainly happy and excited about leaving for the seminary, I too felt tears in my eyes as we pulled out of the driveway and I saw my brothers and grandmother follow the car to the main road. I remember asking God why leaving had to be so painful. It seemed to me that since I was answering His call, He could have made the event a little less painful. Why was it that if you wanted to do something for God you had to give something up and feel such pain?

The trip to Hartford took about five hours. My mother did a great job of getting us there. I felt badly that I wasn't able to help with the driving, for I knew that it must have been very tiring for her. Once in the city we drove down New Park Avenue and there on the right emerged a large, four-story brick building. The sign on the front lawn read, LA SALETTE MINOR SEMINARY. This was to be my home for the next three years.

The parking lot was crowded. Other boys my age were seen dragging their large trunks and suitcases up the outside stairs to the dormitory. Others were kissing their parents goodbye. You could see the mothers drying the tears from their eyes. I wondered if my mother would begin to cry. Finally we found a place to park.

Soon we were walking through the large double doors of the seminary. We nervously followed the signs that directed us to the place of registration. There, at one of the desks, I spotted Fathers Hurley and Jacobson. They motioned for us to come over, and as we made our way toward the desk behind which they were sitting they stood up and gave us a warm greeting. My mother jokingly said, "Well, here he is. You wanted him." And one of them placed his arm around my shoulder and responded, "We'll take him." When they found out that my mother had driven the long distance by herself, they tried to convince her to stay overnight, but she couldn't. She had to go to work the next day.

We were then introduced to one of the seminarians who was to serve as my guardian angel. His name was John Boothroyd. He was a senior and was supposed to graduate that year, but he was later caught smoking and expelled before the year was over. As my guardian angel, it was his responsibility to see that I was properly set up in what was to be my new home. After the registration forms were completed, John escorted us out to our car. We lugged my trunk and belongings up the four flights of stairs to the dormitory. There we found my assigned bed and steel locker. My mother and aunt helped me to unpack. We were then given a tour of the classrooms, the dining room, which they called the refectory, the library, and the areas where I would study and work.

Soon it was time for my mother to leave me. How well I remember the difficult time she had in saying good-bye. How painful it was for her to watch me walk back alone through the large doors and out of her sight. Long ago she told me how she cried during the drive back to Jessup. I was fourteen at the time, and now, when I look at my sixteen-year-old daughter and try to imagine leaving her alone at some faraway school, I more fully appreciate the anguish my mother must have felt. For me it was a day of very mixed emotions. It was difficult to say good-bye and I was worried about her driving home alone. But at the same time I was happy and excited about being in the seminary and beginning a journey that I hoped would lead to the realization of my boyhood dream.

I spent the rest of the day meeting other boys who shared the same dream. Most of them came from Connecticut and Massachusetts. Some of them had just finished grammar school and were even younger than I. They all seemed like regular guys. Later I would find out that that's exactly what they were.

After supper most of us went for a walk around the "track," a large walk-way that surrounded the ball fields and followed the direction of the chain fence that enclosed the seminary grounds. Walking the track each night after supper would become a ritual for me and the other neophytes. As we were walking we heard the clanging of a bell, unaware as yet that it was tolling for us to report to chapel.

Bells, I soon learned, were an integral part of seminary life. They awakened us in the morning, they called us to chapel and meals, they announced the beginning of study hall. At times they came to your rescue by declaring the end of classes, saving you from being questioned on an assignment which was not completed. I certainly heard more bells than Pavlov's dog ever did.

And so, in response to the bell, we entered the chapel for evening prayers. As I looked up to the altar I was struck by the words embroidered in gold on the green altar cover. They read, *Magister adest et vocat te* ("The Master is present and calls you"). I was being called by God, my Master, to serve Him, and I was present in the seminary chapel to answer that call.

After prayers we were told that we would be entering a period called "The Great Silence," no talking allowed until the following morning after breakfast. For those misfortunates who violated the rule, the penance imposed was to take the next three meals on their knees. Many times a good percentage of the student body would be seen on their knees at breakfast attempting to eat soft-boiled eggs, yours truly included.

Most of the time we ate our meals in silence, unless it happened to be a holiday or the feast of some important saint. On those occasions our superior gave us permission to talk during the meal. The reading of newspapers was limited to the sports section. Television was only allowed on the evening before a school holiday, and the program was selected by the superior. Smoking cigarettes on or off the seminary grounds was strictly forbidden, and those who were caught doing so were automatically expelled. Some of those expelled entered other seminaries and went on to become priests.

Not all seminaries were governed by the same rules and regulations as those in my seminary. The regimentation did not faze me. I had expected it, for I believed that self-denial and external discipline helped to build character and would prepare us, as future priests, to resist the temptations of the world. At least that was what I thought at the time. I heard my Master's call and I responded: *Magister adest et vocat te.*

According to traditional Catholic theology, a vocation to the priesthood is nothing less than a call from God to enter into a life dedicated to the service of God and church. Some receive this call at a very tender age and need protection from the world. For this reason minor seminaries were established. In these houses of prayer and study, the tender vocation was nourished and sheltered from the secular world. Here a young boy's vocation would be protected from the world. Here it would grow to maturity and upon completion to ordination would be placed in the world to minister to the needs of Catholic laymen.

Critics both within and outside the church label this sheltered practice as nothing more than brainwashing. However, in the fifties and the early sixties the concept of the minor seminary flourished. Some religious orders had to move to larger houses of study in order to provide adequate room for the increasing number of young candidates for the priesthood. In the mid-sixties, my religious order had to move its minor seminary from Hartford to larger quarters in Cheshire, Connecticut. Today, over twenty years later, I would be surprised to find more than ten such institutions in existence in America. I know that the La Salette Fathers, my former community, has closed its minor seminary in Cheshire.

Most of the closings, I would suggest, have resulted from the fact that the "call" to the priesthood and religious life is no longer being answered by today's boys, for our society has become more materialistic and less spiritual. The words *sacrifice* and *denial* are not found in the vocabulary of today's families, and Catholic parents no longer seem eager to offer their children to the service of God. Moreover, the Catholic church is undergoing some substantial changes, and Americans who call themselves Catholics no longer accept many of its rules and teachings.

I must be honest and admit that my experience of the

minor seminary was positive. Being away from home at such an early age helped me to achieve a healthy level of independence and responsibility. The observance of the many rules and regulations provided many opportunities for developing character and discipline.

We were only allowed to leave the seminary grounds on a few occasions. The father director of the students would give us fifty cents to visit downtown Hartford for a few hours, usually on a Sunday afternoon. There wasn't much you could do with fifty cents, even in those days. Some of us would visit the state capital building or a museum. Others, who lived in the area, would visit their parents, which was not allowed, and obtain money from them to buy cigarettes or magazines. There were a few who met their former girl friends.

Those who were caught visiting parents or girl friends were immediately expelled. These violations were often detected by means of informants or searches of our lockers. While we were attending classes, the director along with his assistant would go through our lockers and personal belongings, looking for contraband. When forbidden items were discovered, such as secular magazines, gum, extra money, or new clothing, the director would question the seminarian as to where they came from, and in most, if not all, cases, the items had been brought from home.

The rule pertaining to relationships with girls was extremely well enforced. Any hint of having a female friend was met with expulsion, no questions asked. After all, we were being trained to accept and live a life of celibacy and total abstinence from sexual relations. Some of the young seminarians never made it through the minor seminary because of associations with females, even if only by mail. Our letters were always censored, and if by chance some lonely young girl missed her seminarian friend and happened to drop him a line, he was dropped from the roster of students.

Fortunately, I hadn't left any broken hearts behind to write to me. However, I did run into a bit of a problem. During one of my Christmas vacations I attended a dance at my former high school, not to dance, but simply to see some of my old classmates and teachers. When I returned to the seminary I inadvertently mentioned this to the director. To my surprise he reacted very angrily. He warned me to never attend such affairs in the future, and it didn't seem to matter that it was a Catholic high school and that nuns were on hand at the dance. You can be sure that I took his words to heart and never again went near a dance or any party where females would be present.

Any seminarian discovered visiting his home during the course of the walk found himself "grounded" for the next two months. He could receive no visits from his parents nor could he leave the seminary grounds. A harsh penalty, but certainly not as severe as expulsion. To the outsider these disciplinary measures may appear to be extremely harsh, and maybe they were. What made them acceptable and bearable was the belief that they would mold us into obedient, chaste seminarians worthy of someday being ordained priests.

I applied myself to my studies and fell quickly into the routine of seminary life. Keeping up with a very full and busy schedule caused the days and weeks to pass quickly, and soon it was time for our Christmas vacation. We were allowed to go home for two weeks during the holidays. When the day of departure arrived I was both happy and sad. Happy to be going home to see my family, because it had been almost four months since I left them, but sad to be leaving what was becoming my new home and family.

It was good, however, to be back home. A break from the busy and regimented schedule of the seminary was most welcome. I looked forward to some home-cooked meals, especially the Christmas Eve dinner prepared by my mother and grandmother. Special foods were served, and as one of our family traditions at the meal, we all dipped bread into honey and my grandmother would place a drop of honey on the foreheads of all the children, the significance being that we should all have a sweet and happy new year. You can imagine my surprise years later when I sat down to participate in my first Rosh Hashanah dinner and found the ritual of dipping bread into honey as a Jewish custom. How distinctively similar.

Most of my short time at home was spent visiting relatives, neighbors, and old friends. What I noticed from all of them was that their manner toward me had become more distant, more formal. It was as if a wall had begun to exist between myself and them. Their speech was guarded, and when slips into profanity occurred their apologies were endless.

I realized that I would have to learn to live with this separation from others. I even felt it with members of my own family. I would be treated differently for the rest of my life. Even today, after leaving the priesthood, I find a difference in treatment and attitude toward me among those who know that at one time I was a priest. There were many times in my life as a seminarian and a priest when I wished and prayed that this "being different" would no longer exist, but I came to see it as just another of the sacrifices required of one who dared to enter the priesthood. And so I eventually learned to accept and live with it.

My first Christmas vacation ended all too soon. It always seemed that as soon as I began to feel comfortable with the freedom that came with being home, the approaching date on the calendar said, "no more." Going back to the seminary in January was very difficult.

As much as I loved the seminary, I always found the pain of separation from my family hard. I especially missed my baby brother. Many a night I cried myself to sleep thinking of him and my family. The shower was always a good place to let out the tears, and I wasn't the only one. I remember feeling utterly miserable. I wondered if seminary life was what I really wanted. Maybe I had made a mistake. I was experiencing a sickness that was spreading through the rest of the student body. Our spiritual director was quick to diagnose the illness as a strong case of "homesickness." This so-called sickness would return many times over the next few years.

In the seminary we didn't have much time to nurse our "illness" or to feel sorry for ourselves. Keeping busy was the treatment offered by the spiritual director, and it was administered in great abundance. In spite of this medication, some seminarians succumbed to the illness and returned to their homes and families.

Before long midterm exams were around the corner and so was Reception Day. This was a very important day for those of us who had entered the seminary in September. Reception Day was always held on February 2, the feast of the Purification of Mary, the mother of Jesus. This was the day that Mary reportedly went to the *mikvah* in keeping with the Jewish laws of purity, which prescribe that upon the birth of a son, the mother is to wait forty days and then present herself for the rite of purification. Of course at the time I was not aware of this Jewish law and therefore never imagined that someday I too would present myself at the mikvah.

The ceremony of "reception" on February 2, 1956, was the first official act by which the La Salette Fathers signified their acceptance of me as a worthy candidate for the priesthood and a future member of their community. It was as if God's call to be a priest was now being ratified by His representatives on earth. We were all assembled in the study hall, and there the director called out the names of those who were to be received. I was thrilled when he called out my name and felt sorry for those in my class who were not accepted. The ranks of my classmates began to dwindle.

My only disappointment on Reception Day was the absence of my family. There was a very bad winter storm and travel was out of the question. During the ceremony I was presented with a black cassock (a long black garment worn over one's clothes) and a small crucifix that was worn around the neck. The crucifix was a small replica of the larger ones worn by the professed members of the community who had already taken vows. Its design was distinctive to the La Salette order; at one end there was a small hammer which symbolized the sins of men, and on the other end, a small pincer, symbolizing penance. And so a very important step was taken on that day. I was moving up the mountain, closer to my goal. Needless to say, I was happy and excited. I proudly wore my religious habit whenever I could and only wished that my family could see me.

All too soon my first year in the minor seminary was coming to an end. It had been an exciting year. Life in the seminary agreed with me. It was also a year of hard discipline and study. A year of no television, except on the nights before a holiday. A year of no newspapers, except for the sports sections. A year of eating most meals in silence. To some it seemed that I had spent the year in a prison, but as far as I was concerned, the discipline was building my character and preparing me for greater sacrifices in the future.

Summer vacations home were always a welcome change. It was good to be with the family and to taste some of the freedom of the outside world. It was an especially happy period for me because I was able to spend so much more time with my younger brother. During my summers at home I worked at a restaurant helping out in the kitchen. The money I earned would be used for clothes and recreational activities. Some of it I gave to my mother. September always seemed to come so quickly and with it my return to the seminary. The pain of separation and the return of that dreaded illness called homesickness announced the beginning of a new year and another step closer to my goal.

Upon my return to Hartford as a senior we welcomed

Gene Barrette into our class. A few years ago the members of the La Salette community elected Gene to the post of superior general. Today he is a parish priest in Georgia. He was to become a close classmate and friend as we continued our studies into our college years. We are no longer friends. We have very separate and distinct life-styles, and the bond that once supported our friendship no longer exists.

My first two years of college were spent in Altamont, New York, a small town about twenty miles east of Albany. The best and most accurate definition of winter is found in Altamont. Snow could still be found on the ground in early May. The college was also a minor seminary of the La Salette Fathers. Virtually all the rules and regulations that existed in the high school seminary were applicable in the college. The one exception was the use of tobacco, but that was restricted to an outdoor location. My time was spent in the study of the liberal arts with a major emphasis on Latin and Greek. The knowledge of Greek would later be employed in the study of Scripture at the major seminary.

My freshman class at this time consisted of about nineteen students. I had begun my journey in Hartford with about fifty-five others, but over the years our ranks had dwindled. However, a new student entered the college seminary that year. His name was Denis Kolumber. He, Gene Barrette, and I were the only ones who made it to ordination. Denis served as a priest in Argentina for a number of years. Since then he has suffered a stroke, and he is now stationed in a parish in Georgia. I located his place of residence and called him last December to wish him well. I have really lost touch with most of the priests I knew while in the seminary and as a priest. This is not rare for one who leaves the priesthood. Till this day I have never been contacted by any priests of the La Salette Fathers. Any contacts have always been initiated by me.

My two years at La Salette College went by rather quickly. Christmas and summer vacations were spent at home, with the exception of the second year's summer. That year I was only allowed to spend two weeks at home, then reported to the novitiate house, located in Bloomfield Connecticut. There I was to spend a year of intense spiritual training; as its culmination I would take the three vows of poverty, chastity, and obedience, thus becoming a professed member of the Missionaries of Our Lady of La Salette.

✳ ✳ ✳ ✳ ✳ ✳

First Vows

It was June, the summer of 1960. There was a presidential election that year and the major political parties were preparing to nominate their candidates for the fall campaign. Most people were quite intensely following the political scene. I was not that interested. I was aware that a Catholic was attempting to secure the Democratic nomination, but I didn't even know his name. My sights were focused on my goal and the next step that would bring me closer to the realization of my boyhood dream. I was now about to begin a year of intense spiritual training. My parents were driving me to Bloomfield, where I would begin my novitiate year.

The word *novitiate* is derived from the Latin *novus*, meaning "new" or "beginner," and the novitiate is a place set apart from the mainstream of everyday life. Our novitiate was located on a farm of about fifty acres, surrounded by trees and hills, isolated from the world. I would be called a novice, a beginner in religious life. It would be a year of probation, and at the end of the year, if I was found to be a worthy candidate, I would be called to become a member of the community through the profession of the three vows.

I was filled with apprehension. In the minor seminary we had heard many stories about the novitiate and how the novices were treated and tested—stories, for instance, of young novices being told to plant vegetables and plants upside down and not being allowed to question the seem-

23

ingly nonsensical orders of the novice master, the priest responsible for their training, discipline, and spiritual development.

Some of the most frightening stories were told of novices being reprimanded in public and humiliated to tears during a spiritual exercise called public confession (not to be confused with the sacrament of confession). This form of discipline was held once a month. It required that you present yourself before the community and, kneeling before the master of novices, loudly and publicly confess all violations of the rules of the community.

Enforced with special rigidity was the rule known as *numquam duo, semper tres,* meaning, "never two, always three." You could never be alone with only one other novice. There always had to be three or more together in a room, on a walk, or working out in the field. I suppose the rule existed out of a fear that particular friendships might lead to homosexual relationships.

Mulling all this over on my way to Bloomfield, I realized that I would soon learn first hand if these stories were in fact true and if the novitiate was really so terrible. In the meantime I preferred to focus my attention on the fact that in order to attain the goal of the priesthood I had to experience the novitiate year. I was also distracted by the upcoming ceremony that was to take place on July 2, also known as Reception Day. On that occasion, along with my classmates, I would receive the official habit of the La Salette Fathers. I would wear the white Roman collar with the black cassock, secured by a cincture which went around the waist and in which was inserted a crucifix similar to the one I had received on Reception Day in the minor seminary, only larger. This was the outfit I would eagerly put on each morning. This was the habit I would wear forever. I felt good in it, very comfortable and proud to wear it. Another step had been taken, and it had brought me closer to my yet so distant goal.

Life in the novitiate was difficult. The rules were many and at times almost cruel. I will never forget the time my parents came with my brothers and baby sister to visit. Once a month you were allowed to have a visit from your family. Visiting hours were scheduled from one in the afternoon till five. While on their way to Bloomfield, my younger brother became car sick and they had to stop for awhile. It was at least a five-hour drive from the Scranton area. On top of that they somehow got lost. They finally arrived at the novitiate somewhere around four o'clock that afternoon. I was relieved and happy to see them.

I felt certain that since they had a legitimate reason for coming so late, the novice master would extend my visiting hours with them; after all, they had traveled such a long distance. He did not. They had to leave at five o'clock along with the other families. They accepted his decision, for they had been raised to respect authority, especially the authority of a priest. And I too accepted his decision as my superior. Today no priest would get away with that. Sometimes I feel angry with myself for allowing him to treat them that way. I should have spoken up for my parents and family, but the times and my own timidity did not allow for a confrontation.

The rules of the novitiate were designed to keep the world and its events outside the walls. Radios and televisions were never allowed to the novices. Nor were we allowed newspapers and magazines except those of a strictly religious nature. The use of the phone was also forbidden, and we were not allowed to accept calls unless it was an emergency. My mother called me to wish me a happy birthday, but the master of novices would not permit me to speak to her. Most meals were taken in silence except for major religious holidays.

Our day would begin early with morning prayers and meditation followed by the celebration of mass. Work assignments would be given out after breakfast, and the morning was spent in completing those tasks. Some of us had to clean out the stalls where the cows were milked. Some of us mended fences, worked in the silo, or bailed hay. There was always plenty of work to do on a farm. At noon we would break for prayers in chapel followed by lunch and then back to our work assignments until the end of the day.

After supper and evening prayers the hours were filled with studying the rule book of the community or reading the life of a saint. At times the master of novices would give us a talk on religious life and suggestions which if followed would help us attain to a spiritual state of life we had never before experienced. I was nineteen at the time, and all of us were young and impressionable. The influence of the novice master over his captive audience was overwhelming. We listened with attentive ears, anxiously awaiting his words of wisdom. Words, we believed, would transform us into spiritual giants like him.

I have never forgotten his first conference with us. The novice master, Father Edward Barry, had been selected because of his deep spirituality and above-reproach reputation. He was a tall man, and his physical stature alone would have claimed authority and demanded respect. In addition, he was a very eloquent speaker who would keep you hanging on his every word. One could listen to him for hours.

Father Barry's first conference with us laid out the blueprint that would ensure our spiritual success. He told us how, during the course of the year, we would be required to carry out orders that appeared to be meaningless. He required our total submission and obedience, and if we gave him that he guaranteed that we would emerge from the novitiate as spiritual giants. He asked that we submit our personalities to him, promising to mold them into the likeness of Christ by the end of the year. We would then be worthy to take the vows of poverty, chastity, and obedience, living sacrifices for the Lord.

During the year Gene Barrette and I constantly compared the progress we believed we were making toward spiritual gianthood. One of the methods used to determine the degree and depth of our spiritual growth was to see who could remain in chapel on his knees, on a wooden kneeler, the longest. Gene always seemed to win.

At another conference the novice master's talk centered around the vow of chastity and the evils of associating with women. Very graphically he described how certain women were just waiting out there to seduce a seminarian or priest. "Put a Roman collar on a telephone pole and these women would flock around it like dogs," he said. Another line from the same talk remains in my memory. "When you hear the clicking of their high heels and smell the scent of strong perfume, run from them," he said. According to Father Barry, all women, with the exception of mothers and sisters, were out to seduce priests and members of religious orders.

Considering how young and impressionable we were, we took his words to heart. We would sit at our desks in awe of this man and nod our heads in agreement. At times we would glance at each other, wondering if we all felt the same way. Later, during our brief recreation period, we would discuss our feelings about him, concluding that he was, no doubt, a living saint.

November, 1960, was fast upon us. I wasn't fully aware of what was happening in the world outside. All we knew came from our novice master or his associates. As novices we were not allowed to speak to other religious members living in the same quarters, other than the "good morning, good evening" salutations. I remember, that November, going in to breakfast after mass and Father Barry granting us permission to speak during the meal, "in honor of the first Catholic elected president, *Deo gratias* [thank God]."

The priests all seemed very excited about the new president. I guess most of the excitement was due to the fact that John Kennedy was an Irish Catholic. Unlike the other members of the novitiate, we novices had not been allowed to watch the election returns the night before. The first time I even saw a picture of Kennedy was when I was cleaning the priests' lunchroom and glanced at a newspaper left on the table. For us novices, the day after Kennedy's election was just another routine day, performing our assigned tasks and religious duties. Later, in the major seminary, I would become a fanatic follower of President Kennedy.

I had been a novice now for over five months, living with the same six novices, and it was becoming more difficult to get through the days. The weather was turning colder and the days shorter, contributing, no doubt, to the depressing atmosphere that seemed to pervade the halls of the novitiate. Christmas was approaching, and this would be my first Christmas away from home and my family.

Father Barry tried to make the event jolly for us, but it didn't work. I couldn't help but think and wonder about my family back home. I missed the traditional Christmas Eve dinner, the good food and cookies that were specially made at this time of year. I wished I could at least call them, but the use of the phone even on this occasion was forbidden. Our dinner that night was like any other night's, nothing special. After dinner we went to chapel for evening prayers followed by a short recreation period. Then on to the study hall till nine o'clock and then to bed. We were awakened at eleven-thirty to attend Midnight Mass in the chapel, celebrated by Father Barry. The highlight of the evening was the surprise cookies and hot chocolate prepared for us by the good nuns. This was a Christmas I would never want to experience again.

Looking back over my months in the novitiate I am inclined to acknowledge that our master of novices did in fact take away our personalities. His influence and the forced discipline of the novitiate dulled our senses and natural curiosity about events taking place in the world. Without external stimuli, such as newspapers, radio, or television, to keep us informed, our minds had no recourse but to consider everything but the novitiate as unimportant and a distraction from the pursuit of our spiritual goals. Our emotions were constantly held in check, and any display of emotional behavior was met with reprimands and even punishment.

Fortunately, I was not content with only the pursuit of spiritual things. Later, as a student of theology and near ordination, I became enthusiastically interested in politics and world events, thanks to the influence of President Kennedy. I believe that this interest in worldly events helped to broaden my mind and increase the focus of my attention to society and the events that were taking place.

I well remember the many heated arguments over the issue of civil rights. Some of the students in the major seminary were from the south and midwest. Most seemed to be opposed to Kennedy's message of granting equal rights to blacks. Some even called him a communist because of his policies and leadership in this area. I believed him to be right and found myself defending his actions before men who were studying to be "other Christs."

I know priests who have never broken out of the mold. They show no interest in the world around them. They are content to follow strictly the rules of the community and church, nor would they dare question authority or take the initiative to make their own decisions. I began to take a different road. Maybe that is why they have remained within the safe womb of the religious community. That may be why they are still priests and I am not.

Somehow I managed to survive the winter. It was good to see the trees turning green again and for the days to be longer. These were signs that soon my novitiate year would be coming to a close. My disposition, along with that of my classmates, began to be warmed by the welcome sun of spring. The only news given us about the outside world at that time was the report of an American invasion of Cuba. To hear Father Barry tell it, war with Russia was imminent and we would probably never see our parents and families again. He seemed to have a flair for the dramatic. Fortunately, the crisis of the Bay of Pigs was not so apocalyptic as he first reported.

The second of July was quickly approaching—the day that would see me consecrate myself to God by taking the vows of poverty, chastity, and obedience. But before this could happen, we novices had to be tested on our knowledge of the vows and the rule of the La Salette Fathers. Our character was also examined to determine whether or not we possessed the spiritual qualities necessary to be a priest and a worthy member of the Congregation of the Missionaries of Our Lady of La Salette.

It is appropriate at this point to tell about the origin of the La Salette Fathers. La Salette is the name of a mountain in the French Alps. In the year 1846, two children, Maximum and Melanie, were tending sheep on the mountainside. They witnessed a brilliant light and upon approaching it saw a woman dressed in the clothing of the region sitting on a rock. The woman, presumably Mary, the mother of Jesus, told them that she had come from heaven to deliver the message that her son was angry with the world and the sins of its people, and, if they did not return to him through penance and prayer, he would punish them with war and famine. A small group of priests, believing the children's story, built a chapel in Mary's honor on the site where the apparition took place. They also set out to establish an order of religious men who would preach this message to the world. The group was eventually sanctioned by Rome and ever since has been known as the Missionaries of Our Lady of La Salette.

And so, having been accepted by my superiors, on July 2, 1961, in the presence of my family and the community, I knelt before the superior and, placing my hand in his, professed the three vows to be lived for a period of three years. I became, at that moment, a member of the community, with the title of "brother" before my name. They became my family and were now responsible not only for my spiritual well-being but also for my material needs.

With the profession of my vows I formally and legally consecrated myself to the service of God and my new family, the Congregation of the Missionaries of Our Lady of La Salette. At the end of three years my spiritual life, character, and level of academic achievement would again be examined by my superiors. If I was again found a worthy candidate, the community would call me to take the same three vows, only now they would remain in force until my death.

But that was to be in three years. Right now I was happy with my current state in life and grateful that I had made it this far. I felt a sense of security and acceptance, and with that I continued my climb up the mountain, hoping and praying that I would make it to the next level and eventually reach the top. Late that afternoon my family and I set out for Ipswich, Massachusetts, where the major seminary was located and where I was to spend the last six years of preparation for the priesthood. Six years to be spent in the study of philosophy and sacred theology.

✻ ✻ ✻ ✻ ✻ ✻

The Last Steps

Profession Day was a beautiful day. The ceremony was solemn and moving. But now it was over and, after a brief reception consisting of cold drinks and cake, we took our place in the caravan of cars and along with my classmates and their families set out for our next destination, the National Shrine of Our Lady of La Salette and the major seminary.

The term "major" was used to designate the school where a candidate for the priesthood undertook the study of philosophy for two years, upon completion of which he received his bachelor's degree and then proceeded with four years of study in theology, at the end of which time he received his master's degree and ordination to the priesthood. During these last four years the seminarian also received his minor orders, a series of steps in which he received certain powers from the church, such as the power of exorcism, which is the power to cast out demons, and the power to read the Scriptures. A total of four minor orders were bestowed upon the candidate during these four years. Today the practice of conferring minor orders has been discontinued. During the time of my studies in the major seminary they were regarded as necessary before one could receive the priesthood.

The drive to Ipswich was a beautiful trip. It was the beginning of July, and all the trees and flowers were at the zenith of their beauty. The scenery seemed to become more beautiful as we drew closer to our destination. I was experiencing a sense of freedom I had almost forgotten existed. To be able to smoke again, to listen to the car radio, to spend so much time with my family made me all the more appreciate the simple and common activities of daily life.

Just being away from the regimentation of the novitiate and knowing that I would never have to experience a year like that again was exhilarating. At the major seminary there would be rules to follow, but nothing like what I had experienced at the novitiate. If you wanted, you were allowed to smoke; wine and beer would be served at holiday meals; radio and records could be listened to during recreation periods and holidays. Television was allowed, although the superior would determine the programs to be watched. Now I could live with that! We would even be allowed to have movies shown on the nights preceding some holidays. I had arrived to enjoy the good life. Life at the major seminary would be bearable, even enjoyable.

Our caravan of cars was now on Topsfield Road, and the entrance to the seminary was only minutes away. We eagerly watched the cars in front of us, waiting to see them turn into the grounds of the major seminary, which had once been an estate belonging to the Rice family. The Rices had donated it to the archdiocese of Boston, and in 1949 Cardinal Cushing, who wanted the La Salette Fathers to have the property, arranged for the archdiocese to sell it to the order for only $100.

Soon the signal lights of the cars in front indicated that we had arrived. Slowly we made the left turn into the driveway. The entrance was marked by a beautiful sign surrounded by red and purple rhododendron trees: WELCOME TO THE NATIONAL SHRINE OF OUR LADY OF LA SALETTE. Beneath that it further read, MAJOR SEMINARY, OUR LADY OF SEVEN DOLORS PROVINCE.

The road wound its way up a slight incline, both sides of it lined with green trees and bright, colorful flowers and plants. As we approached the main house, we saw, on our left, an inviting, man-made swimming pond filled with young boys boating and swimming. They were boys attending the summer camp operated by the seminary and staffed by the major seminarians. The camp was a source of revenue to help defray the operating costs of the national shrine and seminary. It was also a source from which young boys entered the minor seminary. I would spend three of my summers as a camp counsellor, and the fourth summer I would serve as its director.

As we drove further up the road toward the main house, the landscape began to explode with bright, multiple-colored rhododendron plants. The lawn, well manicured and bright green, extended for acres. The grounds were exceptionally beautiful. My family and I could only agree that the reality of the grounds far exceeded the pictures and postcards we had seen.

Soon we began to make out, through the many trees, the outline of the main house, designed as such to distinguish it from the five smaller houses on the three hundred acres of property. These, at one time, had housed the servants, cooks, and chauffeurs who had served the Rice family. The former stables were now living quarters and classrooms for the philosophers, and in the summer were converted into the camp for boys.

Now finally before us loomed the mansion, or as it was called, the main house—overwhelmingly large, dwarfing the minor seminaries and novitiate building. It was hard to believe that this would be my home for the next six years. The mansion served as residence for the priests, each having his own private room, some with fireplaces and private bathrooms. There were about fifteen priests and six brothers. (Brothers were men who professed the three vows and were members of the La Salette Community, but did not pursue the priesthood; their ministry consisted of taking care of the physical tasks of operating the seminary and seeing to the needs of the priests. Some of their responsibilities were quite menial, such as setting the tables and cleaning up after meals. They seemed happy in their calling, perhaps because they believed Milton's words, "They also serve who only stand and wait.") One of the smaller homes on the property housed a group of Italian sisters who prepared our meals and did our laundry. We always looked forward to Thursday's lunch of authentic spaghetti and meatballs.

The chapel, which at one time had been the living room for the Rice family, was located on the first floor of the mansion. Its marble altar was framed within the large fireplace and was truly the focal point of the room. The walls of the main hall were covered with beautiful, carved wood, and at one end was the large and beautiful dining room with its Cara marble fireplace. This was the students' dining room. At the other end of the hall was a large library which now was used as a conference room for the students. Downstairs there were bowling lanes, a recreation room with a television, a barber shop (some of the seminarians were excellent barbers), and a music room where one could listen to his favorite albums. On the fourth floor was the theologians' study hall, classrooms, library, and dormitory. The theologians lived and studied in the main house. The philosophers had their quarters and classrooms in the former stables, each student making his home in what had once been one of the stalls. It was almost like having a private room and was a welcome change from the open dormitories of the minor seminaries and novitiate. There were also classrooms, a library, study hall, bathrooms, and showers. This would be my living quarters for the next two years.

The brief description I have given you in no way does justice to the estate. One would have to see first-hand what I have tried to describe on paper. The numerous pilgrims who arrived by bus to attend the Sunday shrine services were always overwhelmed by the beauty of the place. They especially loved to take part in the rosary procession, which wound its way through the perfumed, brightly colored and manicured rose gardens to the outdoor shrine, where they would be led in prayers honoring Mary and listen to the message of La Salette given by one of the priests who staffed the shrine. During inclement weather the services would be held in the large shrine church.

That first summer I and several of my classmates were assigned to work on the grounds of the seminary and shrine. We would tend to the cutting of lawns and general landscaping. On Sundays, we would assist in the shrine services by directing traffic and people to their designated locations. Our nights were free to watch selected television shows, read, or do practically whatever we wanted within the framework of the rules of the major seminary.

Although we were not allowed to go home for vacations during our six years at the major seminary, we did have a two-week vacation each summer. Divided into groups, we would drive to Lake Winnepausauki in New Hampshire. There we took up living quarters in a large summer house situated on the shore of the lake. The house had been donated for this purpose by one of the wealthier benefactors of the seminary. We water-skied, swam, fished, and in general had a great time. Summer vacations were relished by all, and seemed to strengthen the community bond that united us.

September of 1961 came quickly. The camp was closed and quickly transformed into the home of the philosophers in time for the first day of classes. I would soon find myself in the abstract world of Aristotelian philosophy, the adopted philosophy of Thomas Aquinas and the church. Our classes and textbooks would be in Latin, the official language of the Roman church.

The only philosophy and theology allowed in the classrooms of the major seminary was that of Thomas Aquinas. This closed system left no room for debate or comparisons with other philosophical and theological systems. We were, in that sense, spoon-fed a tried and tested philosophy that supported the many tenets and dogmas of the church. All other philosophers and their teachings, including those of Moses Maimonides, were treated as adversarial and not allowed to be objectively studied or discussed. Their works were not allowed in our libraries, and if it was necessary to read any of their writings, special permission was needed from the superior and the works of the adversary could not be removed from the locked room where such writings were stored. Overall I enjoyed my studies in philosophy and only wished that the classes and textbooks were in English. The Latin caused extra work, since translations were necessary to truly understand the concepts.

Living as a member of the La Salette Fathers provided me with freedom from material needs. I was about twenty-one at this time, and men my age living in the world had to contend with real life and its problems. If they were attending a college they had to worry about paying tuition, room and board. No doubt many of them worked to help defray the costs. Others my age were married and had assumed the responsibilities of being husbands and in some cases providers for their children. I had taken the vow of poverty, but in reality others were living it. I had no material needs to worry about. I never had to pay a bill or a mortgage payment. I ate well and never had to think about where the next meal would come from. I lacked nothing material.

The vow of obedience at this time produced no problems. I followed the daily routine of the seminary and always carried out my work assignments without difficulty. Those in the world lived obedience. Obedience to their bosses at work or suffer the loss of their job. Obedience to their wives and children or live a life of frustration.

Chastity was the most abused of the vows. Thoughts of girls and sex constantly bombarded our minds. We were at the peak of our sexual life. There was a constant battle raging within our bodies. Taking pleasure in an impure thought, as described by Catholic moral theology, was considered to be a mortal sin, even for the lay-person, but for one who professed the vow of chastity it was a sin of sacrilege, a violation of the vow. The consequences of such a violation, should one die in that state of sin, would be eternal damnation in the fires of hell.

The sacrament of confession was the immediate remedy. Usually before morning mass a line of guilty, remorseful seminarians would be found waiting to enter the confessional, waiting their turn to confess the sin and receive absolution from the priest. To act out those impure thoughts was even more horrendous, and the usual advice of the father confessor more disturbing. "It is the devil who is doing this to you. It is his way of distracting you from the goal of the priesthood." And the prescribed cure to help combat these inclinations was, "Play sports! Keep your mind occupied with good thoughts and your body busy with worthwhile projects."

Of course being in bed alone at night didn't allow one the opportunity to carry out these remedies. And of course father confessor never ever indicated or hinted that he himself had ever had or might still have such strong inclinations. So you were left with the belief that if this appetite could not be controlled before ordination, you should consider leaving your vocation. Often, throughout the course of seminary training, the dictum "Many are called but few are chosen" would come to mind at such times. Talks on chastity almost always ended with the words of St. Paul, "Better to marry than to burn" (1 Corinthians 7:9).

Were the seminaries filled with homosexuals? Absolutely not! When people ask me about this I respond that homosexuals can be found in all walks of life, the armed forces, married life, the teaching profession, and in members of the clergy of all faiths; there exists in the seminary and priesthood neither more nor fewer homosexuals than are found in any other profession. What I relate to you here is by no means intended to produce scandal or shock, or to bring shame upon the church. I write candidly of what I know and experienced so that later you can more appreciate why I so eagerly adopted the teachings of Judaism. And here I cannot resist mentioning that in retrospect it seems to me that I did not truly begin to live my vows until, as a Jew, I became a husband and a father. What could a vow of poverty mean to me when I never had to pay bills or provide for children? In those days I never considered providing for retirement, never had to take out a car loan and worry about paying it back. As for the vow of chastity, its full meaning can only be appreciated when one is a married man bound to be faithful to his wife. And insofar as obedience is concerned, I had only one superior to obey and answer to under my vow. Today, I have five, my wife and four children whom I must obey. And I have had superiors at work to whom obedience was due else I would be without employment. I mention this because so often people would say to me back then, "Oh, you poor man, you have to be faithful to three vows. How do you do it?" In comparison to living in the real world, it wasn't that hard.

With the freedom to watch television, I found myself becoming deeply interested in John F. Kennedy, the new president of the United States. I was well into my first year of philosophy, and it appeared that a new wind was blowing not just in this country but also in the Catholic church. A new pope had been elected, Cardinal Roncalli of Venice, who assumed the papal name of John XXIII. Under his pontificate a need developed for seminarians to become more informed about the outside world so as to be better equipped to handle its problems.

My superiors' first step to this end was to allow us to watch the evening news and all current events. This soon became an after-dinner ritual. The recreation room would become a sea of black cassocks and white faces all focused on the screen that would enlighten us with its words and pictures about the world we were all so eager to save. There, one evening, was the new president, sounding strong, appearing leaderlike, taking to task the wealthy heads of the major steel companies for escalating their prices.

I found myself impressed by him and what he said. He appeared to be a true champion of the people. From that time on I made it a point not to miss the evening news, hoping that I would see him again. Like so many Americans I became infatuated with this young president. I wished I would be like him. I soon became one of his strongest supporters in the seminary and often found myself defending his policies and programs over dinner, during recreation, and even during Grand Silence, that period of time beginning after evening prayers and ending after breakfast during which talking was not allowed.

With the new wind blowing we were now allowed to read the entire newspaper, along with copies of *Time* and *Newsweek*. I soon became an avid reader of these periodicals and eventually became the seminary's expert on current events. Because of this influence I began to broaden my outlook on life and began to expand my mind to include secular questions as well as church studies.

I argued, for instance, that priests should be in the forefront of the civil rights movement. Others in the seminary disagreed. A priest, they said, should not take sides on such issues. He is ordained to minister to the spiritual needs of Catholics. Let the civil leaders handle secular problems. These were pretty much the sentiments of the majority of priests and seminarians in the seminary at that time. I believed differently. Unknowingly, the seeds of discontent were being sown in my unconscious. Later, when I was an ordained priest, they would come to fruition and help to form the platform that would direct the thrust of my ministry.

In September of 1963 I entered my second year of philosophy. I was anxious for the year to be over even though it had just begun, for I was eager to enter my first year of theology, the year that would see my class take perpetual vows and receive minor orders. For now I focused on my last year of philosophy. I was soon preparing for the first quarterly exams, which would take place on the days prior to Thanksgiving, beginning on Thursday, November 21.

The exams would be taken in the mornings and the afternoons were spent in work details. Each quarter some major cleaning projects would be scheduled. The wooden walls of the main hall and stairway would be polished, the wood floors waxed and buffed, windows cleaned both inside and out.

On Friday, November 22, I was assigned to work outdoors raking the tons of leaves that were now only reminders of the beautiful summer past. I was riding in the back of one of our large dump trucks filled with leaves. We were on our way to unload them at the dump site. As we turned onto the road leading to the site, I could see Father Carroll, the director of the national shrine, coming toward us blowing the horn of his green station wagon. We stopped and he pulled up next to us, rolled down his window, and shouted those unforgettable words, "President Kennedy has been shot. They don't know yet if it is serious."

My first thought was that he would now surely win his reelection bid, for he would be viewed as a national hero. Quickly we proceeded to empty the truck of its summer remains and hurried back to the main house, rushing down the stairs into the recreation room to see and hear the historic events taking place in Dallas. The TV cameras were sending pictures of Parkland Hospital and the crowd of onlookers. Then we heard a report that was replete with foreboding. Two priests had administered the last rites to the president, a sacrament of the church usually performed on one perceived as dying.

Suddenly Walter Cronkite was on the screen, "President Kennedy died this afternoon!" "No, that's not possible," I thought. He couldn't be dead. I could not accept Cronkite's words. They must have made a mistake, I told myself. But as the reports of Kennedy's death rapidly followed each other, I had to accept the fact of this national and personal tragedy. I ran out of the room to the nearest bathroom and there allowed my hurt the relief it so desperately needed.

The days that followed were spent glued to the television, where I joined the rest of the nation in mourning the loss of my idol. Time was also spent in the chapel attending the many masses that were offered for the repose of his soul. The wounds caused by his death were raw but in time would heal. The emptiness that I felt would last for many years. He had made a profound influence on my life. His vision of a just and better world became mine. He, more than the pope or any other priest, influenced the course that my priestly ministry would take.

I had now moved to the main house and was entering my first year of theology, the study of God's nature. The classes would consist of Sacred Scripture, both the Old and New Testament, canon law, moral theology (the different kinds and degrees of sin), church history, and dogmatic theology (the dogmas of the church, such as the trinity, papal infallibility, and Mary's virginity). This would all be very interesting, I felt, and much more practical than the philosophy of Thomas Aquinas, with its many abstract principles.

The knowledge imparted to us through our study of Thomist theology was, as you might imagine, church dictated and sanctioned. Our study of the Scriptures, for instance, was meant to prove that Christ was the Messiah of whom the biblical prophets spoke. Thus we never read the interpretations of Jewish biblical scholars. To give an example: Catholic scholars claimed that when the prophet Isaiah spoke of a child named Immanuel who would be born of a virgin (Isaiah 7:14), he was referring to Jesus. They never mentioned that Isaiah could have been referring to King Hezekiah (see II Chronicles 32:32), as many Jewish commentators maintain, nor did they indicate that *almah*, the word translated as "virgin" in Catholic Bibles, really means "maiden" or "young woman" and has nothing to do with virginity.

Since all other religions were considered to be in error, there was no need to study their teachings; they were plainly wrong. Only the Catholic church possessed absolute truth, any other interpretation of the Bible was either false or only partially true. The difference between Judaism and Christianity was prejudicially and incorrectly defined in terms intended to show Christianity as superior. The God of the Old Testament, the God of the Jews, was a God of vengeance who said, "eye for eye, tooth for tooth" (Exodus 21:24); He had been supplanted by the New Testament God of love, kindness, and forgiveness, who said, "Turn the other cheek" (Matthew 5:39).

In moral theology we learned about the nature and effects of sin. There were three kinds of sin—mortal, venial, and original. Original sin is the sin committed by Adam and Eve and transmitted to all generations. With the exception of Jesus and Mary, every child born into the world is born with original sin, which can only be removed through the sacrament of baptism. The soul of a baby who dies before baptism is sent to a place called limbo and cannot enter heaven. Venial sin includes relatively small offenses, such as lying, missing prayers, and being selfish. Offenders are sent to purgatory, where suffering from fire will purify their souls of these minor imperfections. Those who die with mortal sin on their souls, such as missing mass on Sunday, having impure thoughts, performing impure deeds, or practicing birth control, are sent to burn in the everlasting fires of hell. Armed with these ideas, reinforced by countless volumes on moral theology classifying every sin imaginable, I would, as a priest, sit in the tribunal of confession and judge the penitents who came to me for absolution.

I am almost always asked if there was any anti-Semitism

in the seminary or in the teachings of our professors, who were all priests. I never heard any seminarian say or do anything that could be called anti-Semitic, but once, when we were studying a tract on why a good God would allow suffering, one of the students asked our moral professor, Father Pius Lutkus, "Why have the Jewish people, who are the Chosen, suffered so much?" Father Lutkus answered, "Because they asked that the blood of Jesus be upon them and their children."

This is known in some Christian circles as the "blood curse." According to the Christian gospels (Matthew 27:15–25, Mark 15:6–15, Luke 23:17–23, John 19:39–40), Jesus was brought before Pontius Pilate, the Roman governor of Judea, to be tried for blasphemy. Pilate could find no guilt in him but was afraid to set him free because it might incite the people to riot. Since it was Passover, and it was customary to release prisoners at that time, Pilate presented Jesus and a thief named Barabbas to the crowd. "Whom shall I free, he asked, Jesus, who claims to be your king or Barabbas?" According to the Christian gospel, the people shouted, "Free Barabbas, free Barabbas." Pilate asked "Then what shall I do with this man called Jesus?" And the people shouted, "Crucify him, crucify him. Let his blood be upon us and our children."

Father Lutkus never mentioned, and perhaps did not know, that the idea of freeing prisoners at Passover was invented by the authors of the gospel. It is totally unsubstantiated in the Jewish legal sources of the time and is regarded as absurd by historians familiar with Roman colonial policies. Instead, he merely summarized the story as told in the gospels and added that the blood curse is why the Jews have been so persecuted and subject to so much suffering, and why they will continue to suffer in the future.

Since we were on the subject of the Jews, another student asked whether they would be saved. According to Father Lutkus, the Jewish people had sinned against the holy spirit by rejecting Christ and could not be saved. A sin against the holy spirit, he explained, was a sin against truth, and such sins, according to Catholic theology, can never be forgiven. The scriptural basis for this teaching is found in the gospel written by John, "He [Jesus] came unto his own [the Jewish people], and his own received him not" (John 1:11).

This is what my classmates and I were taught, but in all fairness, I must point out that such teachings are now rejected by the church. Ever since the Vatican II ecumenical council and the pontificate of John XXIII, the official teaching of the church regarding the Jewish people has clearly stated that the Jews of today cannot be held responsible for the death of Jesus. All disparaging words about Jews in the liturgy and official teachings have been removed. For example, for many centuries the services on Good Friday, the day commemorating the death of Jesus, included a prayer that began with the words, "For the perfidious Jews . . ." Pope John ordered these words stricken from the text. However, this could well be a case of too little, too late.

My next immediate concern was to prepare myself for the reception of minor orders and the profession of my perpetual vows. I had fully expected to profess the vows with my classmates, and thus was dismayed and shocked when the director told me that he, the superior of the seminary, and the first counselor had voted in secret, following the usual practice, and since I had not received the requisite three votes, I would not be allowed to take my final vows this year.

Our director, at the time, was Father Steve Krishanda, who was from my hometown of Jessup. When he told me the news I felt as if my life had ended. I couldn't believe that this was happening to me.

"Father," I asked, "why can't I take my perpetual vows? What have I done wrong or failed to do?"

"John, I don't know what happened. You didn't receive the three positive votes necessary to be called to final vows and minor orders, someone voted against you."

I sat there in disbelief, then began to cry. I was doing well in my studies, my spiritual director had told me that he would recommend me for final vows, why had this happened?

"Who voted against me?" I asked Father Steve.

"I don't know." he replied. "We vote in secret and there would be no way of knowing who cast the negative vote."

Immediately, I knew that it must have been the first counselor, Father LeFrancois. He was also my Scripture professor. I had never felt that he liked me. He was always cold and never seemed to give me due credit for my work in class. But why would he have done this to me?

Of course I didn't learn the truth until much later. Father Loftus, who was also from my hometown and would later deliver the sermon at my first mass, told me that he knew who it was but would not reveal the name until after I was ordained. How he knew who it was I don't know. I only know that it was after my ordination and a couple of stiff drinks that he found the courage to tell me that it was Father Steve who cast the negative vote. By then Steve was serving in the Argentine missions. I felt both angry and very hurt. I never found out why he had voted against me.

The day of perpetual profession arrived. I sat in my place in the seminary chapel and with a broken heart watched my classmates take their vows. My hurt was so deep that I thought of leaving the La Salette Fathers and entering the diocesan seminary in Scranton, but my classmate, Gene, talked me out of it. "Don't worry, John, you'll take them next year and you'll still be ordained with us." He was right. I wasn't required to repeat the entire year. I could take my perpetual vows next year along with minor orders. That thought eased the pain, but the wound was still there.

In September of 1964, I professed the three vows of poverty, chastity, and obedience forever. I was now a perpetual member of the La Salette Congregation. Now I was prepared for the reception of minor orders. The bishop would come to the seminary and perform the ancient rite of bestowing minor orders on this year's candidates, I being one of them. The minor orders consisted of exorcist, lecture, acolyte, and porter. They were in most cases merely symbolic, the order of porter, for example, bestowing on one the power to open and close the doors of the church. Nonetheless, and this was the source of their importance, a candidate for the priesthood had to receive them before he could advance to the major orders of subdeacon, deacon, and finally priest. And so another step was taken which would see me closer to my ultimate goal.

Life at the major seminary was good to me. I had made many friends among the lay-people in the area who often came to the shrine for Sunday services. In a very small way we were being introduced to the world and the people to whom we would minister. The church was attempting to modernize itself and so were the seminaries. A new pastoral program was introduced into our curriculum. Two evenings a week we would teach religion to Catholic high school students in the local parish church.

Teaching provided a great opportunity for us to test the knowledge we had gained from our theology classes. Many times were we disappointed and discouraged. The teachings we offered had no relevancy in the young lives of our teenage students. Often I was shocked when they asked questions I could only regard as sinful about important church teachings.

The times were changing. People were beginning to question authority and tradition in all spheres, religious and secular. The days of demanding and receiving blind obedience were coming to a confusing end. Television was gradually replacing the pulpit and the classroom, its messages eagerly heard and accepted as "gospel truth." Violence, beginning with the murders of President Kennedy, his brother Bobby, and Martin Luther King, was brought into the living rooms of people not only in this nation but across the world. The tragic era of the war in Vietnam brought not only pain and suffering but a soul-searching and questioning of our basic values and ideals.

Not since the days of the Protestant Reformation had the Catholic church been so attacked from within its own ranks. Bishops and prominent theologians began to publicly question the official teachings of the church regarding such major issues as birth control, divorce and remarriage, priestly celibacy, and premarital sex. The ancient, sacred dogmas of the eucharist and the mass were questioned by liberal theologians. Even the divinity of Christ was brought into doubt.

Many Catholics were confused, but in the midst of this turmoil, I continued my traditional studies and accepted the true and tried church teachings expounded by my conservative professors. I intended to remain a staunch defender of Catholic doctrine who would chastise those who confessed the sin of birth control.

I recall an argument I had with a deacon who was soon to be ordained a priest. He asserted that it would not be a mortal sin for a married couple to miss mass on Sunday in order to have sexual relations if it was their only opportunity to be alone together. This, he said, was using their time for a better end, namely, the preservation of their marriage. As far as I was concerned, one was never excused from the obligation to attend Sunday mass, the only exception being illness. To remain home from mass in order to have sexual relations bordered on the blasphemous.

Before long our seminary community broke down into liberal and conservative factions, although it must be said that the individuals in both groups were, by and large, honest, well-intentioned men searching for truth. I could have been described as Mr. Conservative. I didn't want to see the church change anything. I liked and wanted to keep the Latin mass. And as the seminary's choir director I fought against those who wanted to throw out the Gregorian chant and bring in English hymns that had been composed by

Protestants. I loved the church's many rituals and symbols, and hoped they would not be altered or, worse yet, eliminated from the liturgy. Eager to serve as a priest in a church no different from the one I had known as a boy, I resisted, as did many others, the changes that one day would cause me to question my identity as a priest.

In the summer of 1966 I had my first experience of what being a priest in a parish church was all about. In June of that year I was ordained to the diaconite, the last step before the priesthood. As a deacon I was empowered to baptize, distribute holy communion, read the gospel, and preach to the laity. It was a thrill to share so closely in the powers of holy orders.

My two classmates and I were assigned that summer to minister as deacons in St. Joseph's parish church, located in Fitchburg, Massachusetts. Living in the rectory and working closely with the priests there, we helped with the distribution of holy communion at the Sunday and daily masses, visited the sick of the parish and at times brought them the eucharist, preached at the Sunday masses, imparting what we hoped were words of inspiration and wisdom to our captive audiences, and were involved, as well, in cook-outs and the many other social gatherings that keep a parish church operational.

Many a night we found ourselves attending social functions in the homes of major benefactors of the church. Extra attention had to be given to these people. They were the cream of the parish, and I saw the priests stumbling over each other in an effort to make them feel important. This sort of thing began to bother me. The idea of having to cater to the wealthy was distasteful, and as a result my summer at St. Joseph's was spoiled. What should have been a positive experience left me with a disdainful feeling for pastoral life. I made up my mind that I would not serve out my priesthood in a parish church. I had no desire to play the role of politician and glad-hander.

When I returned to the seminary in September, my summer's experience weighed heavily on my mind. Did being a priest mean that I would have to play such a banal role? I had loftier ideas and ideals about what a priest's ministry should be.

For the first time in my life I began to seriously wonder if the priesthood was what I really wanted. I began to suffer periods of depression. I didn't want to speak to anyone. Often I would lock myself in the music room and listen to depressing music. On Sundays I would return to my sleeping quarters as soon as shrine services ended so as not to meet or talk to any of the people who came every Sunday and with whom I had become friends.

Never having experienced such moods of depression before, I was troubled by my behavior and sought help from the spiritual director, Father Abend. Baring my soul, I told him about my summer at St. Joseph's, my moods of depression, and my doubts about becoming a priest. Father Abend sat back in his armchair, pensively smoking a cigarette, and spoke in a fatherly tone. "John, you know, what you are feeling are normal fears of one who is shortly to become a priest." He continued, "The devil would like nothing better than to be able to steal a vocation from God. You are being tempted by him to reject the call."

His words were soothing, and in his firm but quiet way he helped me to feel good again about the priesthood, assuring me that I had a true vocation. With Father Abend's help I refocused on my goal, which was now only seven months away. Everything would be all right, I told myself.

What with my improved attitude and the news that my two classmates and I would be moving to one of the servant homes to take up quarters, the problems of the summer rapidly disappeared from my mind. Having my own room, with its own door, would be a welcome treat. After having spent the last eleven years in a dormitory, this was going to be fantastic. The year was shaping up quite well. It would be my last year as a student. The top of the mountain would soon be mine. The long journey was finally coming to an end.

Behold The Priest

Never in my boyhood dreams could I have imagined the joy that filled my heart when I heard the words, "Thou art a priest forever, according to the Order of Melchizedech." And then felt the hands of the bishop pressing firmly upon my head, as two thousand years of tradition magically transferred the priestly powers of ordination to my being. At the moment of the laying on of hands I became a Roman Catholic priest. The dream of my youth had been realized.

The morning of ordination day came early for me because of the excitement I knew it would bring. It was Saturday, May 27, 1967. After thirteen years of study and intense discipline, after thirteen years of perseverance and hard work, the day of my ordination had arrived. I remember looking into the mirror as I shaved and thinking that the ordinary young face it reflected would soon become the face and person of "another Christ." From that moment my soul and being would be transformed. I would be marked with the indelible sign of the priesthood.

After dressing, I walked down to the main house to meet my parents and family and to have breakfast with them. My parents, three brothers, and sister along with my grandmother, uncles, and aunts were there waiting for me. My parents were overflowing with pride and joy. After breakfast they presented me with a beautiful silver chalice, the inside of which was inlaid with 24-karat gold, to be used at my mass and hold the wine that I would consecrate into the blood of Christ.

Ordination to the priesthood is the most essential of the seven sacraments of the Catholic church, for without it the Catholic faith would cease to exist. Without the priest there could be no sacrifice of the mass, no eucharist, no sacrament of confession. A man has the spiritual power to consecrate ordinary bread and wine into the body and blood of Christ, reenacting for the believer the most sacred of mysteries, the Last Supper of Christ.

To think that within a few short hours I would receive the supernatural power to transform bread and wine into the body and blood of Christ was overwhelming. In addition I would receive the power to absolve sin from the souls of penitents, taking the place of Christ in the confessional; I would also receive the power to bless people and objects, to perform marriages, and to preach and teach with the authority of the Roman Catholic church. Indeed, through the rite of ordination I would become "another Christ."

The time for the ceremony was fast approaching. I left the main house to garb myself in the sacred priestly robes and take my place in the procession forming at the rear of the shrine church. There we waited, and soon the procession began down the main aisle, ending at the steps of the high altar where Bishop Reilly of the diocese of Boston stood waiting. As the procession neared the steps of the altar, I could clearly see the bishop, dressed in his majestic robes, waiting to confer the sacrament of holy orders upon my two classmates and myself. The fact that only three of us were left out of the fifty-five who began at the minor seminary filled me with a tremendous sense of accomplishment. I had reached the top of the mountain.

The bishop was a frail, elderly man, kind and warm in appearance, yet eliciting a degree of filial fear and respect. Upon reaching the steps of the altar we prostrated ourselves before him. As I lay there on the cool, marble floor, my head resting in the crook of my arm, I could hear the seminary choir begin chanting the Litany of the Saints, a prayer invoking the saints and holy men and women of the church to intercede for us before God. *Kyrie eleison* ("Lord have mercy"), chanted the choir.

As the choir continued with the names of the saints, I could feel my heart pounding in my chest and a throbbing in the temples of my head. I wondered if I would make it through the ceremony. The choir continued, *Mater Dei, ora pro nobis* ("Mother of God, pray for us"). I began to think of the irrevocable step I was about to take. I felt a sense of finality, of no turning back. Feelings of unworthiness began to plague my mind. My human frailties suddenly loomed larger and larger. A sense of loneliness overcame me, as if I were about to be removed from the world even as I was being ordained to save the world. I would be called father, but would never have children of my own. I was sacrificing myself to God and the church. I was becoming a visible sign of a kingdom that was yet to come, the Kingdom of Heaven.

A loud clap from the hands of the master of ceremonies signaled the end of the litany. It also served as our cue to rise from our prostrate position and kneel before the bishop. The choir was silent, and the church and its congregants became still. The moment of my ordination was here.

I knelt before the bishop and he whispering told me to bow my head. I waited to feel his consecrated hands on my head. Then it happened. His hands pressed firmly upon me, and at that very moment of the laying on of hands I became a Roman Catholic priest. The joy and happiness I felt at that moment would not be experienced again until the day I held my firstborn in my arms. Again I knelt before the bishop. He anointed the palms of my hands with holy oil, consecrating them as sacred instruments with which to offer the sacrifice of the mass.

I began to grasp what had just happened when my parents approached the altar after the ceremony ended and knelt before me. I raised my arms and traced the sign of the cross over my mother's head. "May almighty God bless you. In the name of the father and of the son and of the holy spirit. Amen." I extended the palms of my hands, now emanating the sweet smell of the oil of consecration, for her to kiss. Then I bent down and lifted her from her knees to kiss and embrace her. I thanked her for helping me to realize my dream. In like manner, I blessed my father, the members of my family, and the friends who had come to witness my elevation to the priesthood.

May 27, 1967 was a day that witnessed the dream of a young boy come true. A day that at times had seemed so unattainable, so elusive. Now it had become a day never to be erased from my life.

My First Mass

The plane began to make its descent, and as we circled Avoca Airport, an old poem taught me by one of the nuns came to mind. I had often recited it to myself when the going got a little tough. I don't remember the author's name, but somehow I felt it was mine:

Boyhood dreams of long ago, saw an altar fair.
Consecrated trembling hands lifted there in prayer.
And those dreams have led me on, dreamlike though they
    seemed.
Now dear friend, thank God with me, for I am what I
    dreamed.

It was hard to believe that I had made it through those many years of study and hard discipline. To think that out of so many other, more intelligent, more pious boys, I was one of three who reached the altar. And now I was coming home to share this joy with family and friends. The plane landed, and there in the terminal were my parents, eager to take me home.

For every newly ordained priest the thrill of celebrating his first public mass in his home parish is only surpassed by the thrill experienced on the day of ordination. This most often takes place a week after the ordination ceremony. During this week, the newly ordained celebrate mass but not for the public. You might say that the week is used as dress-rehearsal time, for no matter how much you practice, mistakes will occur, due mostly to nervousness. I was no exception to the rule. The mass is a reenactment of the sacrifice and death of Jesus, and in performing it the priest is, according to Catholic theology, performing a miracle that more than anything else confirms and realizes his identity as a priest. How could one not be nervous?

All the way home from the airport we passed familiar sights that brought back memories of my boyhood. St. Patrick's High School reminded me of the good nuns who had encouraged my vocation, and I wondered if any of them were still around. Later I would make it a point to call upon them. Soon we entered Jessup. My dad drove up the main street. I could see the old familiar buildings. Mr. Mandel's auto supply store, the old movie house that was now a dress factory, and many other childhood landmarks. When we passed the parish church a feeling of pride and accomplishment came over me. On Sunday I would be celebrating my first public mass in the building where I had been baptized and served as an altar boy.

The closer we got to home, the more anxious my mother became. She'd had our house remodeled for the occasion, and this would be my first time seeing it. For a moment I thought it was the wrong house, it looked so totally different. Mom had really outdone herself this time.

As we turned into the newly paved driveway the rest of my family came out to greet me. It was good to be home with them. It was Friday, June 2. Tomorrow I would visit the parish priest, Father Dlugos, and go over last-minute details with him for the celebration of my mass on Sunday.

Tonight, however, I would relax with my family, look at old pictures of when we were all kids. My brothers and I would recall stories of our boyhood and just have a good time. I especially enjoyed the pictures and stories of my younger brother and sister. I had missed their early childhood since I had not been allowed home during the past six years. Soon it was time for bed. I went to my old room and there knelt by my bed, trying to find the words that would appropriately thank God for all He had given me. I had left my home and family as a young boy and returned an ordained priest.

Saturday morning I went to visit Father Dlugos. This was the man I had looked up to with awe when he distributed our report cards in school. This was the man whose mass I had served as an altar boy. Now we shared equally in a brotherhood of priests, but I would still call him father. My respect for him was too great, and in that he was superior to me.

Father Dlugos and I went over last-minute details with the choir director and master of ceremonies. Afterwards we had lunch. Then he surprised me by asking if I would like to hear the children's confessions at two o'clock.

This was my first time in the confessional as a priest, and I was very nervous. I entered the confessional, placed the purple stole around my neck, and opened the sliding panel to hear a child's voice begin, "Bless me, father, for I have sinned." And so they all confessed the same minor offenses you would expect from children. "I called my brother a bad name. I answered back my parents. I said a bad word."

Later in my priestly ministry I would hear and forgive the sins of adults. Not bad people. Good, honest people who happened to be simply human, confessing their human weaknesses. The confessional always offered me the opportunity to play the role of father-confessor. It felt good to make others feel good. To be able to forgive them their sins and have them leave the confessional in a state of grace made my role as father-confessor worthwhile and fulfilling.

Later that afternoon I returned home because I had received special permission to say a mass there, the permission needed because normally one is not allowed to celebrate mass in a private home. Some of our close friends and neighbors had been invited to celebrate the liturgy with us. As I was preparing the kitchen table, it struck me that it was the very same table on which I had played mass as a child. Now I would again be celebrating the mass on the kitchen table, only this time it would be for real.

Sunday, June 4, 1967, finally arrived. We were all up very early, getting ready for a day of solemnity and much happiness. This mass would be a solemn high mass, which meant that the assistance of three other priests would be required. My cousin Father Ruby, a Franciscan, would serve as my deacon. Father Joe Loftus, an old friend of my parents, would act as subdeacon and later would deliver the sermon. Father Dlugos would serve as the arch-priest. My youngest brother, Charles, would be the main altar boy.

The procession formed outside the church and proceeded through the main entrance. The church, with red and white carnations decorating the altar, looked beautiful, and then the organ and choir bellowed out the powerful Latin hymn, *Ecce sacerdo, magnus* ("Behold the great priest"). Walking down the aisle I saw many old friends and former classmates, and felt like a small-town hero receiving the accolades of its residents.

My parents, especially my mother, were filled with pride and happiness. To be surrounded by so many relatives, friends, and neighbors who came to see your child perform such a wondrous miracle was one of the happiest days of their lives. "This is the day which the Lord has made, let us rejoice and be glad." As I was lifted up by the priesthood I raised my family with me to a new social status in the parish and the town. They were now regarded as being on an equal footing with those families who boasted of having a doctor or a lawyer as a son.

When the ceremonies at the church were completed we went over to the parish hall for a wonderful dinner. Later that afternoon a reception in my honor was held in the same hall, and it seemed as though all the town's residents came.

It was a long day for us, but one that brought much joy, love, and happiness, a day honoring not only me but my parents and family.

Whenever I think back on it, however, I marvel at God's mysterious ways. Here I was performing the sacred liturgy of the Catholic eucharist. As part of the ritual I had accepted the gifts of bread and wine brought to me by my sister Maria and my cousin Annmarie. Raising the bread, I had said the required blessing, "Blessed art Thou, Lord our God, King of the universe, Who brings forth bread from the earth." And in like manner a blessing over the chalice filled with wine, "Blessed art Thou, Lord our God, King of the universe, Who creates the fruit of the vine." Would anyone have dreamed that one day years later I would be saying the very same words over a kiddush cup and *hallah*.

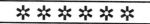

My Ministry

With the celebration of my first mass behind me and a wonderful week spent with family and old friends, I boarded the plane at Avoca. As I settled in for the hour or so flight, I began to wonder what my superiors had in mind for me to do as a newly ordained priest. What would be my first assignment? I hoped that I would be allowed to work at the national shrine in Ipswich. I wanted to continue to develop the youth programs there.

As I contemplated what part of the world I would save, one of the stewardesses asked if she could sit next to me. I was somewhat embarrassed. She was fairly attractive and I worried about how the other passengers on the plane might view the situation. Not wanting to appear rude, I told her it would be okay. She introduced herself as Ann and said she was from Buffalo, New York.

My hands were sweating from nervousness. I had never sat so close to a young woman, and I found it very difficult to relax. I kept wondering if this was the kind of woman our superior of novices had spoken about in his talk on chastity and women. Her questions seemed normal.

"Are you a real priest?" she asked.

"Yes, as a matter of fact I was just ordained. I was home for the past week to celebrate my first mass," I responded.

"How come all the good-looking guys are either married or priests?"

That seemed to be more of a statement than a question that needed an answer. At any rate, I certainly didn't have an answer. I was beginning to feel more uncomfortable. Was she going to sit with me during the entire trip? Maybe she wanted me to hear her confession.

Ann told me she was a Catholic but not a practicing one. She couldn't accept the church's teachings on such matters as birth control, divorce, and remarriage. She used to go to church when her schedule permitted, she said, but now no longer attended because of the changes in the mass. She liked the Latin and the ancient rituals.

Well, at least we agreed on something. Our conversation for the rest of the trip stayed on the subject of religion and why priests don't marry. I assumed that she was just curious about me and saw an opportunity to corner a captive priest who was not going to yell at her for questioning the church or for not going to mass.

Just before we began our approach to Logan Airport, Ann excused herself and went to the front of the plane to prepare the passengers for landing. When she completed these tasks she returned to the seat next to me. She asked for my phone number and in turn volunteered hers.

Giving her my number was a mistake I would pay for during the next few months. She would call me at the seminary whenever she could, telling me how much she missed me and on many occasions inviting me to visit her at her apartment in Revere. My superior began to wonder about the phone calls, and some of the other priests began to tease me whenever another call came in.

I thought that in time Ann would leave me alone. I didn't want to hurt her feelings by being mean to her. However, when she started sending me cards signed "love," I knew that the only way to put an end to this one-sided romance was to be firm and leave no doubt as to where I stood. I must admit that I did like the idea of being loved by a female stranger; it was new to me, and it was an emotion I had never experienced before. I set about doing the right thing. I wrote Ann that I was very happy in the priesthood and told her that her phone calls would not be accepted. I guess seeing my intentions in writing finally convinced her that there was to be no future with me. And so I never heard from her again, and, I confess, I missed her calls.

Ann aside, it was great to be back at the seminary in Ipswich, living as a priest. So much more freedom was allowed me than I had experienced as a seminarian. I was assigned a room with its own fireplace (in working condition). Television was available in the recreation room whenever I wanted it. I had my own radio and played it whenever I wanted. I decorated my room as I pleased. I enjoyed the music of the Supremes and hung a large poster of theirs on one of the walls.

Not all the priests shared my taste in music, especially my former spiritual director, who was next door to me. Some didn't like the fact that I had a poster of "niggers," as they so blatantly called the Supremes, hanging on my wall. I would in time find out, to my disappointment, just how human and vulgar priests could be. Later, there would be confrontations with them. For now, I was happy being a priest and tasting the freedom that came with it.

As I explained earlier, I had taken a vow of poverty, but believe me when I tell you, I didn't live a life of poverty. My clothes were purchased in expensive stores and were paid for by the treasurer. I couldn't have told you in those days what an invoice looked like. The meals prepared by the nuns were fantastic, especially on holidays. The liquor provided us was of the best labels, and the quantity was more than sufficient. And if we got tired of eating in, we would get permission from the superior to take one of the cars and head out to one of the many fine seafood restaurants in the area for a superb lobster dinner. On many occasions, when it came time to pay the check, some generous benefactor of the church would insist on taking care of it, as though attempting to perform a *mitzah*.

Similarly, if we were standing in line to purchase tickets for a show, we could always count on the manager's bringing us ahead of the line or on some Catholic layman to offer us his place. Nor would you be likely to find a priest in traffic court to pay a fine for speeding. Once, for instance, while driving over the speed limit on the Massachusetts Turnpike, I was motioned to pull over by a state trooper. When he realized I was a man of the cloth, he simply advised me to drive within the limit but did not issue a warning or a ticket.

For whatever reason, I found that wearing the Roman collar entitled me to a special treatment not enjoyed by people in many other professions, religious or secular. Personally, I found this embarrassing. I didn't feel that I should be treated so differently just because I was a priest. In spite of my many objections, Catholic people apparently felt that being extra kind or nice to me was their way of showing their deep respect and admiration. So I learned to live with this and to accept it as part of being a priest.

When the year's assignments were posted on the bulletin board in our recreation room. I saw, to my extreme delight, that I was to be one of the assistants at the national shrine, specifically charged with operating the youth programs. These included the Youthquake program, geared to high school students; programs for local college students; and the Newman chaplaincy at Salem State College and the Beverly School of Nursing.

This was just what I wanted to do. It was a ministry I felt I could best serve, for I liked working with young people. I enjoyed their honesty and openness, and respected their desire to be socially active Christians rather than being just "Sunday Catholics." They were eager to serve their fellow man and wanted someone to show them how religion could become the vehicle of their acts.

I was in tune with them. For me religion, more specifically,

Christianity, called on us to be concerned with all of society. I sought to model myself after the example of Christ, whom I saw as having been totally devoted to serving others; angels or sinners, it didn't matter.

And so, armed with these truths I found myself involved with those who needed physical as well as spiritual healing. I saw a need to help young people who had become afflicted with the habit of drug abuse. The sixties witnessed the beginning of this scourge, which has still in no way diminished. I sought to work with and to counsel these young people regardless of the time of day or night.

Many times the demands of this ministry took me away from the comforts and brotherhood of the community to which I belonged. As a result, conflicts arose between myself and my superiors. They were not very happy with what I was trying to accomplish. Maybe they didn't understand what I was attempting to do or maybe they didn't see any need for a priest to be involved with drug addicts. One thing is certain: they did not appreciate young addicts coming to the seminary to visit me.

Some of the teens, it is true, looked like hippies, but I was trying to help them overcome a serious problem and, unlike my superiors, realized that their appearance was merely a superficial symptom. Most of the young people I dealt with were sincere, honest, basically good kids who were emotionally incapable of solving their own problems. I found in many of them a sense of resentment directed at their parents or some other authority. Not able to handle their bad feelings directly, they had turned to drugs for relief.

I remember one young man in particular. He was about eighteen and was using LSD. He would come to the shrine once or twice a week to see me. One morning he arrived quite early, went into the chapel, which at that hour was filled with priests and seminarians preparing for mass, and began shouting, "Where's Father John? I need him."

I was not there, since it was my week to celebrate mass for

the Maryknoll sisters living in a convent about ten miles away. When I returned to the seminary, my superior called me into his office. "John, you just can't have these kind of kids coming here anymore. They are disruptive to our life."

"In what way?" I asked.

"Well, the young man who came to see you this morning rushed into the chapel yelling for you. Then he walked up to the altar and in front of all present began to disrobe himself. We had to have him thrown out."

I later found out that he was experiencing what was known as a bad trip. I felt awful, especially when I discovered that he had left his prized flute for me. About two weeks later an elderly man came to see me. He met me in the front room and began to weep. He was the father of the boy who came shouting for me, and he was crying because he had just committed his son to a mental institution. LSD had destroyed his young mind; he was only eighteen.

"Why didn't you tell me he was on drugs? I didn't know he was doing that," the father cried. I could almost feel the hurt in his heart. I had promised the young man that I would not tell his family that he was on drugs; now I felt sick that I hadn't informed them. Could his deterioration to the point of requiring commitment have been my fault? If I had contacted his family, they would at least have had an opportunity to get help for him. I had deprived his father of that consolation. The father thanked me for trying to help his son, but I knew that in his heart he held me responsible for the tragedy that had struck his family.

The tragedy which befell this boy and his family affected me deeply. I began to question my involvement in a ministry that demanded not only an attentive ear but medical and psychological understanding which I did not have. It seemed to me that if I was to continue working with addicts, I would need the support of professionals with the necessary expertise. To this end, I suggested to my superiors that we convert one of the five homes on our property into a halfway house with a staff that could help young drug addicts.

Needless to say, the suggestion was not accepted. It was one thing to put up with seeing these "characters" every once in a while, but to have them actually stay on the seminary grounds was out of the question. I tried to argue my case but to no avail. I found that I would have to limit my involvement with these young people.

It was extremely difficult for me to go back to the kids and tell them that we couldn't use the facilities on the seminary grounds. As a priest I represented the Catholic church in their eyes. The church was supposed to be the epitome of Christian charity, concerned primarily with helping others. Now, it was, in effect, turning its back on those who needed its consolation the most. Why couldn't my superiors see this?

This incident made me realize that there was a conflict between what the church said and what the church did. I began to see this conflict reflected in any number of other incidents, and in consequence began questioning not only the authority of my superiors but their very belief in Christianity.

A case in point: when I returned to the seminary after my first public mass at home, one of the first questions my superior asked was, "John, where is the money you collected from your mass and reception?"

At first, I didn't know what he was talking about. "What money, I don't know what you mean."

"You know, the money that people gave you as a gift at your reception," he responded.

"Oh, that money. Well, I let my mother keep it so she could pay for the affair. I don't even know how much money there was."

This was the truth. I had assumed, and so did my mother, that the money we received could be used to pay for the expenses involved in the celebration of the first mass. There was a lot to pay for: the flowers, the caterer, the invitations, the rental of the hall. If my mother had had to pay all this out of her own pocket, it would have been a real hardship.

Well, I thought my superior would have a stroke. "What," he yelled, "you gave the money to your mother? That wasn't your money to give away, that money belongs to the seminary. Your parents were supposed to pay for the affair!"

This kind of thing happened again and again. Very often I would be called upon to marry some of the young adults. Many of them were not financially stable, and I disliked the idea of taking money from them. And so I would not accept the gifts they offered.

"Please Father, take it."

"No," I would reply, "you guys are going to need it more than I or my community."

And they would thank me over and over. "You're a good priest," they would say.

That statement meant more to me than any gift of money they could have given. However, you-know-who did not appreciate my so-called indiscretion. Again I would hear, "You can't give that money away, it belongs to the community. You used one of our cars to get to the wedding, didn't you?" he asked. "Yes," I answered. "Well, we need the money to pay for the gas and the wear and tear on the car."

Admittedly, the order had expenses, and I could almost agree that he was right. But when I saw how we priests foolishly and lavishly spent the money of those who sent in donations to support us, I felt more than justified in what I did. We had not only a large quantity of liquor on the premises, but all of it was of the best quality. Sunday nights were called *gaudeamus* ("let us rejoice"). All the priests and brothers would gather in the recreation room, eagerly waiting for the superior to arrive with the trays of deli, party snacks, and most of all booze. There was never any limit as to how much you could drink, except your own.

This was considered "community night," a time to share

in the joys of brotherhood and family, a time to be with your fellow priests and members of the community. Many were very "community-minded." In the beginning of my priesthood I shared in this sense of community and learned well the art of imbibing. Later I would not attend these gatherings on a regular basis but would spend the time with people who needed the services of a priest. In time I was criticized for not attending these community get-togethers and for not being "community-minded." These developing seeds of discord later caused me to consider leaving community life and becoming a parish priest.

Many situations arose during my years as a priest that put me in a position where I had to choose between ministering to the faithful and spending time with the other priests. Allow me to relate one such incident. It was the Fourth of July, and the superior was planning a big community cookout. The menu consisted of barbecued steaks, shrimp, and lobster, all of which were my favorite foods, and I was looking forward to the affair. Around four in the afternoon the phone rang. I ran down the hall to answer it.

"Good afternoon, La Salette Fathers, can I help you?"

"Please," a woman cried on the other end, "I need a priest to come over right away. My husband is very drunk and wants me to get him a priest. He wants to confess his sins but isn't a Catholic. I am a Catholic, but I don't belong to any parish. Can someone help me?"

I took down her name and address and assured her that I would be right over. I took one of the house cars and drove the short distance to Beverly, the neighboring town where she lived. A very distraught woman met me at the door and led me into the living room to meet her husband. He was in a chair, his head nodding in sleep.

"Maybe I should come back."

"No, I'll wake him," she said.

He was a very big man and appeared to be quite drunk. "Sit next to me," he commanded.

Being eager to please I drew up a chair and sat down. He wanted first to know if I was really a priest. He said I looked too young. I assured him that I was. He indicated that even though he wasn't a Catholic he wanted a priest to hear his confession. I told him that it would be perfectly okay. I was too frightened to deny his request.

The stories he began to relate about his life were enough to make me want to get out of his house as soon as possible. He was a "soldier" for the Mafia, and he gave me a full account of his life of crime, including the victims he had killed and how he had disposed of the bodies by transporting them up to New Hampshire and dumping them in an isolated lake. At times he interrupted his confession to threaten my life if I ever repeated what he was telling me. I assured him that as a priest I was bound by the seal of confession and could never reveal the sins of a penitent no matter what consequences I would have to face.

I felt by now that it was time to get out of there. It was pretty late; besides, I was scared. But he wouldn't let me go. He was about to have dinner and I had to be his unwilling guest. Several times, during what I felt was my last supper, he raised a knife to my throat and swore that he would kill me if I ever divulged what he had confessed.

I began to seriously believe that I would soon be joining his other victims on the bottom of a lake somewhere in New Hampshire. I was never so frightened in my life. Finally, thanks to his wife's intercession, I was allowed to leave. I jumped into my car and headed for the safe haven of the seminary. It may have been my imagination but I could swear that I was being followed by a black limousine until I finally turned into the seminary driveway.

It was so late when I got back that the July Fourth celebration was over. The superior came upstairs as I was placing the car keys on the rack outside his room. Without even asking where I had been, he began to lace into me for missing the cook-out. "Everyone was there but you; I guess you're not willing to share yourself with the members of your community." I explained where I had been and how close I had come (at least in my mind) to being killed, but he continued admonishing me about the importance of community life.

By this time it was becoming evident that my superiors did not accept my view of the priesthood and community life. I felt that I had been ordained to serve others, and that the community was there to nourish and sustain me in my ministerial endeavors. I had not become a priest to live a sheltered life within a community of other men. I had not become a priest to watch television all night and keep others company to dispel their loneliness. The conflict between the ministry of the priesthood and the obligations toward the community grew deeper and more difficult. At times I believed that I would never find a resolution to this conflict. But for now I would continue the work I so much wanted to do.

One of the assignments I found very rewarding was that of the campus ministry. I served as Newman chaplain for Salem State College and as chaplain for the Beverly School of Nursing. It was the latter part of the sixties and the campuses were busy trying to find solutions to the many problems afflicting the nation, including the war in Vietnam. At one time I had supported the war, but later I became one of the many voicing opposition to our nation's involvement in the Far East.

I followed the campaign of Robert Kennedy closely. He was not Jack, but his ideals and charisma were close to those of his slain brother. He seemed to enjoy much support on the college campuses and in particular at Salem State. Efforts to aid him on what we hoped would be his journey to the White House were in full stride when, to my horror and disbelief, I awoke on that June 4, 1968, to hear of his assassination.

My immediate reaction was one of disbelief. It seemed

unbelievable that Bobby too had been violently slain. I drove over to the college to help the many students who were shattered by the news of his death. I felt their sorrow because it was the same grief that I had experienced only five years before. I prepared a memorial liturgy for the slain senator and celebrated a sorrowful mass in a chapel overflowing with young mourners. The task now was to pick up the pieces of their shattered dream and channel the energy of these young people into good works. The senator had often spoken about reconciliation, and so programs were begun that had the reconciliation of all people as their goal. Black and white, Jew and Gentile prayed and worked together to make our society a better place in which to live.

Around this time I worked on an ecumenical service with the Protestant and Jewish chaplains, our first attempt at an ecumenical event. Both were sincere, honest men of God who also devoted much of their time to the needs of the students. We found through this service that there was more uniting us than dividing us. Certainly the Protestant would never accept the papacy with all of its Roman trappings, and certainly the Jew could not accept the divinity of Jesus. But all three of us accepted and believed in the fatherhood of God the Creator, the One God. And we all accepted the Ten Commandments given to us by the one Law-giver. In these beliefs were we one and united.

Working with these men opened my mind to at least acknowledge that there was much that was true in their religious creeds. No longer could or would I consider myself a herald of the only true religion. Because of my friendship and association with the other chaplains, I began to question church dogmas that at one time I would have defended to the death.

I learned from both of these men to go to the Scriptures for truth rather than to my theology manual. And as I began this practice I found myself becoming more Christian and less Catholic. I began to rely more upon my own interpretation of the Scriptures than on the teachings of Rome. I began to approach pastoral problems, not armed with my book on moral theology but guided by the question, How would Christ have resolved this problem? Thus, for instance, I asked myself what Christ would have said to a Catholic penitent who found it necessary to practice birth control but wished to remain in the church.

Birth control was a vexing problem not only for Catholic lay-persons who had to decide whether to practice it but for me and many other priests who sat in the confessional and had to administer the church's harsh judgment against those who confessed such a sin. Our moral theology professor had told us that birth control was evil and had branded those Catholics guilty of it as evil, selfish individuals.

"Remember," he would say, "if penitents won't renounce this sin and won't promise to avoid it in the future, you cannot grant them absolution from their sins and they are forbidden to receive the sacrament of the eucharist," meaning that they could not receive communion with their children at mass. I knew of such a case where the couple's son was receiving his first holy communion. Because of their need to practice birth control they could not receive communion with him on that day. I wonder what reason they gave him for their lack of participation in the sacrament.

As a young theologian I subscribed fully to my professor's instruction and the teaching of the church on this subject. I saw birth control as a sin against natural law, the violation of which resulted in a mortal sin exacting eternal damnation as punishment. I upheld this teaching because it was and still is regarded as an official teaching of the church, and therefore can never be changed even by the pope, since he is not above natural law.

During the sixties this teaching came under constant attack by liberal theologians, but the church remained adamant and would make no exceptions. Applying my rule, "What would Christ do in this situation," I concluded that

God would not condemn people who in legitimate circumstances used birth control devices. Such people were not evil
and selfish, as my moral professor claimed. They were
sincere Catholics who loved their church and wanted to stay
in its good graces.

I could no longer defend the traditional teaching on this
subject. It was extremely painful not only for the penitent
but also for me. I had seen too many leave my confessional
without receiving absolution for their sins, some absorbed
by guilt and sorrow, others angry and frustrated. Rejecting
the church's natural law argument, I told those who confessed the sin of birth control to follow the dictates of their
conscience. If the circumstances were such that birth control
was their only recourse, then they should feel free of any
guilt or sin and continue to receive the sacraments.

Most penitents appreciated this approach, but not all of
them. I recall a woman who confessed the sin of birth control
to me. I said to her, "God understands your situation at
home. He does not condemn those who try to live within
His law. He does not demand the impossible from us. If you
believe in your heart that you and your husband are doing
the right thing, then no sin has been committed."

Her voice shattered the silence of the confessional and the
church. "You should not be allowed to wear the Roman
collar," she screamed at me. "You are not a true priest of the
Catholic church. You were ordained to teach and uphold the
laws of the church. What right do you have to tell me that I
haven't committed a serious sin?"

I sat there in shock and embarrassment. I couldn't believe
what I was hearing. Who was this woman, and why was she
so angry with me? She stormed out of the confessional
before I could respond. There was nothing I could do for
her, so I continued hearing the confessions of the other
penitents. Her words, however, distracted me from giving
them the full attention they deserved.

That night, when I told some of the other priests about

this incident, their reaction was, "Don't let it bother you, John. There are a lot of crazy people out there." Father Welch added, "Maybe she was one of those penitents with a very scrupulous conscience. I've had a couple of them myself."

Whether she was crazy or whether she had a scrupulous conscience didn't matter to me. The woman was actually right in what she said. I was a Catholic priest, and as such I represented the teachings of the church. What right did I have to place my opinion above the teaching authority of the pope and church? No rabbi can take it upon himself to change the halakhah all on his own.

I had to be true to myself and my conscience, and at the same time I had to be true to what I represented. And so a conflict of tremendous proportions began to plague my life. I tried desperately to resolve it, but to no avail. I was on a dangerous course. I could not accept the church's teaching on birth control. And this rejection ultimately led me to question and doubt one of the church's most fundamental teachings, one upon which my Catholic faith existed, namely, the infallibility of the pope and of the church's teaching authority.

With this burden on my shoulders I continued with the ministry assigned to me. The youth programs at the shrine grew rapidly. Busloads of high school children would be heard coming up the main road, shattering the silence of the seminary grounds. Looking out their windows to find out where all the noise was coming from, some of the older priests were startled by the sight of hundreds of teenagers running up the walkway that led to the shrine church where the famous Youthquake program was to be held, all of them eager to hear and participate in the now acceptable and permitted guitar mass or folk mass, as it was called.

To help me administer the program and handle the large groups, the director of the students gave me permission to employ the services of some of the seminarians. They supplied their musical talents and were a hit with the young participants. I supplied the talks and homily, heard confessions, and officiated at the celebration of the folk mass. The objective of the program was to present the teachings of Christianity to young people in terms and language that were meaningful to them, often using popular Beatles songs as a vehicle or medium.

The program was very successful, and before long it was well known throughout the North Shore area of Boston. The next logical step was to extend it into a two-day affair, with one of the servant homes converted into living quarters for the young participants. The weekend program was called a Youthquake Retreat. At last, I thought, I had convinced my superiors to make good use of the physical resources located on the vast seminary grounds, and I looked forward to the new program getting off the ground.

And then I learned that another priest had been named director of the program. I felt slighted and hurt, since it was my idea and an extension of the programs I was currently operating.

I approached Father Carroll, the director of the shrine and my immediate boss. "John," he said, "I tried to get you the assignment, but they were concerned that you might take advantage and begin to use the facilities to house drug addicts and runaways."

"Tom, that's not fair. You know how hard I worked to get them to allow these weekend retreats. It doesn't seem fair to assign the director's position to someone who really doesn't care about or believe in the program."

I was very angry. But nothing was going to change. Within a short time the program failed. I think they wanted it to fail. I could see that my three years at the national shrine were coming to an end. The conflicts between my superiors and myself were not going to be solved. If anything, they became more intense.

I involved myself in my priestly ministry, seeking out those in need rather than waiting for them to call for help when it would already be too late. As far as my superiors were concerned, they would have been content to have me perform my daily chores at the shrine office. These duties involved a daily trip to the post office to pick up the mail. Afterwards, I would sit around a table with the shrine director, his assistant, and one of the secretaries. We would open the envelopes and empty them of the financial contributions sent in by benefactors both poor and wealthy. Then we would read the letters. Some would write of their hardships and ask for our prayers. Others would tell of their health and financial problems. Still others asked for prayers to be said to convert a husband from alcoholism. It was like reading a litany of all the problems people had to encounter in the world. There was, no doubt, a ministry involved in simply responding to them and offering them some hope and consolation.

After lunch it was back to the office. Time would be spent in sending out mass cards and bottles of miraculous water from the site of the apparition in La Salette, France. The work at the shrine office would end with a final trip to the post office to mail the precious bottles of holy water and the letters bearing words of hope and encouragement for those suffering souls in the world.

Late in the afternoon the bell would summon us to chapel for vespers, followed by supper. A quick dash to the community room to watch the evening news and then back to chapel for evening prayers. Afterwards some priests would retire to their rooms, others would return to the community room for a night of television.

Yes, my superiors would have been quite happy with me if I had only been content to follow the rest of the community's schedule. Going out to local parishes on weekends to help with confession and to say mass was enough to fulfill one's priestly duties. What more was needed? This was my superiors' idea of how a good, community-minded, La Salette priest should live. It was not mine.

My nights were often spent taking an alcoholic to one of his meetings or counseling a spouse at ALA-NON. I also worked with the children of alcoholic parents in a program called Ala-teen. What a tragedy for these young kids to have to witness their parents almost constantly drunk. Many evenings I spent in trying to comfort and find shelter for abused women. Often I would beg my superior to allow one of the homes on the property to be used as a shelter for such women and their children. And, of course, I was involved with my campus ministry and the youth program for high school students.

My superiors decided to transfer me. After three years working at the national shrine and six years as a seminarian, I would be leaving Ipswich. My new assignment would bring me to our house of studies in Washington, D.C., where I would attend classes at Catholic University in order to obtain a master's degree in counseling. Once that was accomplished, they told me, I could return to Ipswich and continue the ministries I had begun. I might even be able to use one of the houses as a center for runaways or battered wives. So while I felt sad about leaving Ipswich and the many adults and kids I was working with, I consoled myself with the thought that the separation would not be forever. Someday I would return. But that was never to happen.

The frame of mind I was in at the time was not helped by the atmosphere in Washington. The physical condition and location of the house of studies left much to be desired. It was located on Monroe Street in the North East section of the city, about six blocks from Catholic University. Next door to our house of studies was a very active firehouse.

I had spent the last nine years living in a mansion surrounded by plush, rolling lawns and acres of beautiful trees. Now I would take up residence in a crowded, three-story building surrounded by miles of concrete and noisy traffic. The physical differences alone could cause me to fall into a state of depression.

The house served as a makeshift seminary for La Salette students who were attending theology classes at Catholic University. This was a relatively new experiment at the time. My initial studies in theology had been taken in the major seminary, in a closed environment. But now, in the era of the ecumenical council, it was argued that students who attended an outside college might be better prepared to serve as priests.

Father Andrew Greeley had gone much further, suggesting that seminarians be allowed to attend co-ed parties and events, and even be allowed to date. He argued that this would give them a better understanding of women and a deeper appreciation and respect for their needs. At the seminary in Washington the students were not allowed to date, but socializing with girls was not discouraged. Parties were allowed, and girls from the university were invited. A far cry from my days as a student of theology.

Other than myself, there was one other priest at the house, and that was Father Felix, the superior, who had been my professor of dogma at the major seminary. I enjoyed his company, but his current situation added to my demoralization, for he was seeing and dating a girl, and their relationship had become so serious that they were entertaining the thought of marriage. Eventually he did leave and get married.

The new superior of the residence was Father Avitable. A young man, in his forties, he assumed the role with relish. He was well received and liked by the seminarians, and sought to run the house much like a democracy. He actively sought the advice of the residents on matters relating to its operations, and the students were very much involved in the decision-making process. I was supposed to be his assistant, but I could see that my suggestions and position meant little. He did not need my help or advice.

After thirteen years of studying for the priesthood, I didn't relish the idea of sitting in a classroom again, but I resolved to make the best of it. I missed Ipswich, but Washington was, after all, a very exciting city. At night some of us would head over to the local college hang-out for pizza and beer. I was beginning to feel like a student. I was about thirty at the time and living the life of a twenty-one-year-old. I guess this period spent in Washington could best be described as making up for lost time. I had never had the opportunity to enjoy campus life or, in general, the life of a college student. Now I was making the best of it. Maybe living here in Washington wouldn't be so bad after all, I thought. I attended my classes daily and made every effort to do as well as possible.

My ministry as a priest now was minimal. Some weekends I would go out to Andrews Air Force Base to help the chaplains there with Saturday confessions and Sunday mass, and I did some volunteer work at Providence Hospital, visiting the sick, hearing their confessions, and bringing them holy communion. On one occasion, I had the surprising experience of giving communion to the famous actress Helen Hayes. That certainly made my day. Other than this I did nothing that helped to reinforce my identity as a priest. I could just as well have been another student in the house or social worker. The fire and zeal of my priesthood was slowly diminishing. I was fast approaching a crisis of identity and faith.

The End of a Dream

If someone had asked me back then whether I was a conservative or a liberal, I would have responded: conservative regarding the church's traditions, rites, and liturgy, and liberal in theology and social values. That would have been an honest assessment of what determined my behavior later on.

I was always deeply moved by the rich, beautiful symbols and rituals of the church. The fragrance of burning incense mingled with the scent of burning candles evoked an image of the church that was warm, mystical, and at the same time powerful. It was always a thrill to don the ornate vestments before celebrating the mass. The sacred clothing reminded me of who I was and of the great mystery I was about to perform. And what more mystical language should this liturgy be spoken in than Latin, the ancient language of the church.

Rituals has always played a very important role in religious and civic life, for we humans seem to have a need to express our most intense religious and patriotic feelings through rites and symbols. And so, like many other Catholics, I was distressed by the many sweeping changes brought about by the liturgical reforms of the sixties. The "new mass" celebrated in English seemed to lack the mystery and miracle. These still existed because of my faith but were now not as intensely felt or seen by my mind and body. The mass was

becoming a banal event, sometimes even performed without
the use of liturgical vestments, no longer possessing its
former majesty and splendor.

More disconcerting was the fact that my belief in the real
presence of the body and blood of Christ began to waver.
My desire to celebrate mass diminished to such a degree that
its daily celebration no longer seemed important or meaningful. The daily mass had always been a source of identification
and reinforcement of who I was, but this was no longer so.

The new liturgy greatly reduced the once-active role of the
priest. At times I viewed myself more as an observer of the
mass than as the chief celebrant. The first part of the mass
was now given over almost entirely to the laity, with the
priest, referred to as the "presiding president," required to
sit in the "president's chair" while selected members of the
congregation performed rituals once reserved for him. I
sometimes felt that if I had gotten up and walked out, no
one would have noticed my absence. The emotion the mass
had once evolved for me was now supplanted by feelings of
resentment toward the church and toward those who were
stripping me of my duties as priest and principal celebrant
of Catholicism's most cherished rite.

Maybe, in spite of my knowledge of theology, my faith in
Catholicism was rooted more in the powerful rituals, and
symbols of the church than in its teachings. In any event,
the love I once had for the mass was now no longer present
in my life. The daily thrill of celebrating the liturgy was now
replaced by indifference. As a result, I said mass only when
necessary, specifically for the seminarians living in the
Washington house when the superior was not available. The
font from which I had drawn the strength that sustained my
priesthood was now empty.

The void in my heart was filled by a desperate quest for
knowledge about the substance and message of the Roman
church and Christianity. Questions I should have asked
years before now filled my mind and urgently needed satis-

faction. This approach, I soon found, was not enough to save my priesthood and my faith. Somehow the theology of St. Thomas and the church no longer seemed practical. It didn't address the needs of the faithful it had been commissioned to serve by its founder. It was either unable or unwilling to resolve the painful issue of birth control. Its approach to human sexual problems was simply to reduce them to a choice between total abstinence and the eternal fires of hell. The plight of the innocent party in a divorce was worsened by the church's teaching of no remarriage and a life of celibacy or suffer the penalty of excommunication.

In the eyes of the church, human frailty always required a punishment. How could the church claim that her teachings as regarded such matters were infallible, absolute, and binding? According to Catholic doctrine, the church's teachings on morality came with the authority and guidance of Christ, but if so, where was the compassion, love, and forgiveness of the Christ of the gospels, the one who had defended the woman taken in adultery against those who would have stoned her (John 8:7)?

Furthermore, if the church was wrong about birth control, and I along with greater intellects than I believed it was wrong, then it was possible and conceivable that the church could also be in error regarding other teachings on faith and morals. The church and the pope, I realized, were not infallible. The church did not have a monopoly on truth.

Thus if the findings of my conscience were contrary to what the faith demanded, how would I ever resolve this self-imposed dilemma? I sought the advice of some trusted priest friends. Most felt as I did.

"Well, then," I asked, "how can you continue to serve in the church?"

Look, they rationalized, the church is big enough to allow for differences of opinion. Catholics can remain Catholic even if they practice birth control.

"But are they true, practicing Catholics," I asked, "would

the pope sanction their way of life?" It seemed to me that he would not, and they agreed.

I asked them, "Would you remarry a divorced Catholic in the church?" Sure, they replied, the church's teaching needs to allow for exceptions, and in due course that will happen. In the meantime it's not fair to penalize divorced people.

I couldn't believe that my friends actually understood what they were saying. In a strange way I was jealous that they were somehow able to reconcile their rejection of the church's authority with their existence as priests and teachers whose authority came from the very authority they rejected.

I wasn't capable of such rationalizations. If I had been, I might still be a Roman Catholic priest. The gulf between the beliefs of my conscience and the infallible teachings of the church was never to be bridged. I would have to make a decision soon, but first I turned to prayer for help and guidance.

Throughout my life I had always directed my prayers to Christ, to Mary, and to a host of favorite saints. Now I found myself plagued with doubts about Mary's role as mother of God and about the divinity of Jesus. I tried praying, but the words leaving my lips did not represent the feelings deep in my heart. What was happening to me, I wondered. How could someone whose entire life had been one of faith now be so beset by doubt?

Questions and doubts plagued me daily. Maybe I had become too involved with the so-called new theology, which focused more on Christ's humanity than on his divinity. The dogma of the incarnation had always taught that Jesus was both God and man, but emphasized his divinity over his humanity. Now the pendulum was swinging the other way. But the more human Jesus of the new theology was no longer the Jesus I had known and loved as a young boy. He was not the redeemer of my sins, and he was not the

Messiah. The Jesus of my boyhood and the early ministry of my priesthood was eluding me. My theological problems were bringing to an end my boyhood faith in a god who became a man.

✳ ✳ ✳ ✳ ✳ ✳

Starting Over

It was 1971, President Nixon was entering his second year in office. The war in Vietnam was escalating, and so were the protests. The economy was entering a recession, and this too contributed to the unrest that steadily grew during this time. I was entering my second semester at Catholic University. The classes were interesting and I learned much about counseling techniques, but I wasn't happy sitting in a classroom. I felt as though my entire life was coming apart before my eyes.

Doubts about the church and my belief in Jesus continued to plague my mind. I attempted to find solace and help from my community but instead found resentment and isolation. My relationships with most of the students at the house of studies were strained. Maybe they sensed that I wasn't happy there or pleased with the way the house was operating.

To tell the truth, I couldn't blame them. I didn't fully participate in their form of liturgy or their communal activities. They were students while I had been a priest now for almost four years. We were all members of the same community through our profession of the same vows, but we had different interests. Their days were filled with theology classes at the university and their evenings were usually spent in study or socializing. The only other priest in the house was the superior, Father Avitable. He was a wonderful guy, the students loved him, but for some reason we never became close friends and our relationship remained on a professional level. Thus I was very much alone and began to find comfort in heading down to the local pizzeria for some afternoon beers. The frequency of visiting this place increased and so did my drinking. Its effects made me feel good, and in it I found relief from my tensions. I knew this behavior wasn't good for me. If I didn't find a way out of my conflicts soon, I would become too engulfed to heal myself. I had to do something.

Father Cox was now the provincial superior of the community, the ultimate local authority. I decided to ask him to let me return to the national shrine in Ipswich and resume my previous ministry. Maybe going back and immersing myself in work would heal the wound in my faith and save my priesthood. I placed a call to him at his headquarters in Bloomfield, Connecticut.

"Hello, who's this?" he asked.

"Hi Father, it's John Scalamonti."

"How's it going down there? How are your classes coming along?"

"Okay," I responded, "I'm calling to let you know that I want very much to come back to Ipswich in the fall. I miss the work I was doing there. There isn't much for me to do here as a priest. I feel that I'm wasting my time."

There, I had told him. Now I held my breath waiting for his response.

"Well," he began, "maybe that could be arranged. I'll talk it over with Father Carroll and the other members of the council. I'll get back to you in the spring when we decide on new assignments. Regards to Sunny [Father Avitable's nickname because of his happy disposition] and the rest of the students."

I felt great. I was sure that Father Carroll would want me back on the shrine staff. He and I had always gotten along very well, and the two priests on the council were both old friends of mine. Father James Lowery was from Scranton and had been my Latin professor in the minor seminary. Father McWeeney had been my director when I was a theology student in Ipswich.

Filled with hope, I didn't mind finishing the semester at the university and even planned to return at some later time to earn my master's degree in counseling. Returning to Ipswich, I was convinced, would enable me to regain the faith I had lost. Everything would soon be all right again.

A few months passed. It was either the end of April or the beginning of May. I was summoned to the phone one day to take a call from Father Cox.

"John," he asked, "have you decided what you want to do in September?"

I couldn't believe it. Had he forgotten our phone conversation a few months back?

"I thought I would be going back to Ipswich in the fall," I answered.

"Well, we think it would be best for you to continue your studies and remain in Washington for another year."

"Why," I asked, "doesn't Father Carroll want me back at the shrine?"

"Well, we have Father Nowinski there, and he seems to be doing a fine job. There would be no need to transfer him, and we can't afford to have the two of you doing the same job."

I don't remember exactly how the conversation ended. I was devastated. I was furious. I decided to ask for a leave of absence.

In spite of my serious doubts about the church and the divinity of Christ, I wanted to save my priesthood. I was in a desperate state. Without my priesthood, wounded as it was, what else could I be! I was dealing not only with matters of my faith but with my survival as a human being. Was there life for me outside the walls of the seminary?

To strengthen my case when I put in my request for a

leave of absence from the La Salette Fathers, I began looking for a temporary position with the secular clergy. I met with the priest of a church in the Washington area and told him of my current state of mind. He offered me work at his church as director of religion classes for the parish's grammar and high school students. In addition, on weekends I would assist him with confessions and the Sunday mass. The salary was enough for me to live on my own, which was important, since I did not want the community to pay my way.

With employment assured, I summoned the courage to tell Father Avitable about my decision to take a year's leave of absence from the community. He said he was sorry that I had to go to such an extreme but hoped it would be for the best. He urged me to call upon him if I needed his assistance.

Now the curtain lifted for the next act. The stage was set, the script was written, all that was needed was for the players to walk on to the stage and play out their roles. The phone rang three or four times.

"Hello, La Salette Novitiate, may I help you?"

I recognized the voice of Brother Fred. "Hi, this is Father Scalamonti, Fred, could you put me through to the provincial?" I almost passed out from the anticipation and anxiety that filled me at that moment. I almost wished he wouldn't be in.

"Hello, John?"

"Yes it's me, Father. I'm calling to let you know that I've come to a decision regarding my current status."

"Go ahead, what is it?"

"Father, I'm asking you to grant me a year's leave of absence from the community. I have a job lined up with one of the parish churches not far from the seminary. They will pay me and the community won't have to provide me with any financial support during this time."

"Wait," he said, "did you talk to Avitable about this?"

"Yes, I did, he told me to call you."

"And what will you do at this parish church?"

I told him about the ministry they had offered me and that I would be happy doing it. There was a long pause.

"Listen," he said, "I'm not going to grant you any leave of absence. I'll call that priest and let him know that you are forbidden by us to take the job. The only leave of absence I'll grant you is one from the priesthood."

I suppose he said this to bring me back to my senses. My heart jumped to my throat. I wasn't exactly sure what it meant, but it didn't fall within my current plans.

I asked him, "What does a leave from the priesthood involve?"

He replied that a leave from the priesthood would mean that I could not say mass, administer the sacraments, wear the Roman collar, or in any way look, act, or function as a priest.

"That's not what I want, I just want to spend some time away from the community while at the same time observing the life-style of the parish priest first-hand. I'll have an apartment close to the seminary, and I'll still be in touch with them."

He was adamant and would not discuss my proposal. "No, I'm not going to grant your request."

Feeling as if I had been backed into a corner I struck out, "Okay, then, I'll take a leave from the priesthood." I didn't want this, but I felt there was no choice, I was literally fighting for my spiritual and physical life.

"I'll be in touch with you to let you know what has to be done. Good-bye."

I hung up the phone, trembling inside. What had I done? What would I tell my mother and family? I can't remember what I did immediately after the call. My state of mind and being were too confused and shaken.

Days passed and by now most of the students at the seminary knew what had transpired between the provincial and myself. The few who were friends tried to console and support me, but no one could bring peace to my troubled mind. This was my personal crisis and I had to see it through on my own.

A week or so later Father Avitable called me into his room. "Listen," he said, "Father McWeeney called. They want you to fly up to Bloomfield and meet with them."

I guess that was good news. It would be better to meet with the provincial, and maybe he would be more receptive to my request. Besides, as I mentioned earlier, I knew his two counselors. Maybe they would change his mind.

I prepared for the trip in the hope that they would be able to help me through my crisis. At Bradley Airport in Hartford I was met by Father McWeeney. He drove me to the provincial's headquarters but gave no indication of how he felt about my request. He never even asked me why I wanted a leave of absence. Instead he talked about the good old days at the major seminary, where he had been director of students during my last three years of theology.

Father McWeeney was known throughout the community as a tough, conservative, closed-minded individual. Along with being our director he also taught canon law at the seminary. Under his directorship many students either were expelled or left on their own. He was a man who lacked the ability to be flexible, and at a time when the winds of change were blowing so strongly in the church, flexibility seemed to be the key to survival.

I had generally gotten along with Father McWeeney but recall having one major confrontation with him. Because of it I came very close to being denied ordination to the priesthood. It happened in my last year of theology, a few months away from ordination. Two female students from the catechism class I taught came to see me one Sunday without calling first. I was surprised to see them in the lobby of the main house, and the jeans they were wearing made me nervous. I knew the director would not appreciate their attire. The visit was totally unplanned; they had been riding around and on the spur of the moment had decided to stop in to see me.

I quickly ushered the girls into the conference room and closed the sliding door, leaving it open just a bit. One of them wanted to talk to me about a problem. She began telling me about her feelings and attraction to other girls, and her fear that she was becoming a lesbian. As she went on with her story, such things as her dropping in unannounced and her jeans no longer mattered. What was important was the fact that she needed help and had come to me.

Suddenly the sliding door opened and there stood Father McWeeney. He didn't say a word. With his hands on his hips he gave me his all-too-familiar infamous stare. I knew I was in for it. Then he said, "I'll see you later."

I continued my discussion with the girls in spite of the major distraction. When they left, Father McWeeney summoned me to his office. No sooner had I placed one foot over the threshold than he began his tirade, accusing me of imprudence, rashness, poor judgment, and a total disregard for the rules of the seminary. He was livid. "I'm going to take you before the provincial and his council and ask them to deny you ordination to the priesthood." He continued, "You should never have allowed those girls to stay. Their dress was totally improper, and if you had good judgment you would have sent them home to change their clothes."

I tried to tell him my side of the story, but it was impossible to get a word in. Finally, I shouted, "You can take me before the provincial and his council, I'll even go before the pope. One of the girls has a real problem and she needs help. I don't care if she was naked!"

I couldn't believe I had stood up to him like that. I guess I was totally convinced that what I had done was right. I could see how frustrated he was with my response. He dismissed me and for weeks ignored me and would not speak to me.

He never followed up on his threats. In time we were once again on speaking terms.

Today Father McWeeney was driving me to meet with the provincial and council. As we approached our destination my insides began to shake. How would they receive me? Would they grant my request? I was sure of only one thing: the future course of my life might well be decided by today's meeting. I was quickly ushered into the conference room, where I paid my respects to the provincial and took my seat at the end of a long table. At the other end sat the provincial and the two members of his council, Father McWeeney and Jim Lowery.

I began to pour out my doubts and the reasons for the unhappiness that had found its way into my once tranquil life. I told them what I believed could be an avenue for me to take: either an assignment at Ipswich or a one-year leave of absence from the community. I don't think they were even listening to me. They heard my words but not the pain and confusion behind them. Maybe they didn't want to.

Judging from some of the questions they asked, and the solutions they proposed, I knew that they did not really understand what I was saying. Father Lowery, in whom I was very disappointed, sarcastically asked if I was planning to live in an apartment to prove that I could cook for myself. The provincial suggested that an assignment to a parish in England might bring me to my senses. This would have required that I remain in England for six years, and I was not prepared to leave my family for so long a time. Father McWeeney threw out another proposal, "How about going to one of our parishes in New Hampshire as an assistant pastor, that would give you an idea of parish life."

Not one of the three made any effort to help me to resolve my doubts about the church, the divinity of Christ, and community life. They seemed eager to simply apply a band-aid on my spiritual wounds, hoping that it would stop the bleeding of my soul for the time being. Their suggestions seemed to indicate that as far as they were concerned, the best way to handle my crisis of faith was to get me out of their sight. Meeting with them was no help at all. They did not set me on the road to spiritual recovery. Moreover, they ruled that I was not to return to Ipswich and would not be granted a leave of absence. I had two choices: remain in Washington and continue my studies at the university or request a leave of absence from the priesthood.

I didn't stay for lunch. Brother Fred drove me to the airport to catch the next flight to Washington. The next few hours I can only describe as time spent in hell. I felt lonely, dejected, frightened, full of despair. What was I to do? If I left the priesthood, how and where would I live? How would I earn a living for myself? What would I tell my mother and family? A million questions flooded my mind, but for now there were no answers.

I arrived back at the seminary in Washington only to walk into an empty house. I was very upset that none of my friends were there for me to talk to. I walked down to the pizzeria hoping to find some of them, but no one I knew was there. I ordered myself some beers, hoping to escape from my problems. While sitting there I tried to pray, but I wasn't able to find the words. I knew now that my faith in Christ no longer existed. I felt that even he had abandoned me and maybe had never been there in the first place. I would now have to rely solely upon myself.

One thing was certain: I had to leave the Washington house. I would begin by finding a place to live and a job. Wait a minute! Did I say get a job? What kind of job could I get? All my years of study and preparation had been geared to the priesthood; what could an ex-priest do in the world? The position I had lined up with the parish priest was no longer available, my provincial had seen to that. Now I would have to find a real job in order to live in the real world.

I began to look through the help-wanted section of the *Washington Post*. There I found an opening for a guidance counselor and teacher at a prison. Certainly I could qualify for that. I called for an appointment and in no time had an interview. It went quite well, and I felt confident that I had the job. I don't remember what it was paying and I don't remember asking about benefits, I had never had to concern myself with such matters.

Next I began searching for an apartment. I still wanted to find a place near the seminary so that I could keep in touch with my few friends. I found a one-bedroom apartment that rented for $120 a month, including utilities. That sounded manageable. Everything seemed easy enough. I had a job and a place to live. I was all set to begin a new life. I would remain at the seminary until I got my first paycheck, and then I would move to my new home.

While I was still at the seminary, one of the students told me that Father McDermott would be moving in for a short while until he could find himself a place to live. Jim, I learned, was planning to leave the priesthood in order to marry the sister of one of the other priests in our community. I was very surprised. I knew Jim and also knew the girl he was planning to marry. When she and a friend had visited Washington a year earlier, I had spent some time showing them the sights, but she had never mentioned that she and Father McDermott had marriage plans.

I was eager to see Jim and tell him about my situation, as "misery loves company." When he arrived we went out to dinner. Emerson's Steak House on K Street was our destination. Noted for its salad bar and all the complimentary beer you could drink, it was the seminarians' favorite eating place. Whenever guests arrived at our house in Washington, we would take them there.

Over dinner I told Jim about my situation, and he told me about his. He'd been dating for some time and had finally decided to seek a dispensation from his vows in order to marry. Later, I attended his wedding, which was performed in a church by a priest. Jim believed strongly in the church.

He simply wanted to marry. After a while Jim said that he would be willing to pay half the rent if he could stay with me until he got a job. I eagerly accepted. It would be good to have company, and it would sure help to have someone to share expenses.

Events seemed to be going my way, but then the director of social services at the prison called to tell me that the federal government had cut its funding for the program in which I was supposed to work. As a result, the job I had been promised no longer existed.

I was terribly disappointed and felt trapped. I renewed my job search, but the country was headed into a recession and there wasn't much available. One Sunday, looking through the classified ads, I noticed that Emerson's Steak House was looking for waiters, waitresses, and bus boys to work in their new restaurant in Bethesda, Maryland. I decided to apply for a bus boy's position; after all, I knew how to clean tables and sweep floors.

I went to the open-house interview and while filling out the application decided to apply for a waiter's position. I knew they made good money. The woman who did the interviewing was quite pleasant and helpful. I guess she felt sorry for me because of my background. She told me I had the job. The only major requirement was that I wear black pants, black shoes, and a white shirt. Well, that was one requisite I would have no problem in filling. As you can imagine, I had enough black pants and shoes to last a lifetime.

Jim and I finally moved out of the seminary to take up residence in our apartment. Later that week I reported to the restaurant in Bethesda. I was thirty-two years old, a priest who had always been waited on by others. Now I would literally "serve others." When I arrived at the restaurant I was introduced to Tony Tullamello, the assistant manager. He knew about my background, as did the other employees. He had once been a seminarian but had left after only a few years of study, so we had a lot in common. Tony trained me in the art of waiting on tables and became my first friend in what I now considered my new life. He was a good trainer, judging from the tips I collected during my first days on the job.

That night, as I left the restaurant for my apartment, I found myself flooded with mixed emotions. I was excited about the possibility of taking care of myself. Waiting on tables was not the greatest job, but for now it would provide me with enough money to eat and pay my bills. The new-found freedom of living on my own was exhilarating.

On the other hand, I felt a great lack of direction and focus in my life. I blamed God for my current situation and questioned His existence. I wondered why He had abandoned me. I felt anger and resentment toward my former religious superiors.

In addition, I was very concerned about the reaction of my mother and the rest of my family. I did not want to hurt them, but at the same time I had to do what I believed was right for me. They were well aware of my problems with the religious community, and my mother had supported my decision to seek a leave of absence. She knew that I was not happy in Washington and that I had not been alllowed to return to Ipswich. When I told her that I would be living in my own apartment, she responded, "You do what you have to do." My whole family supported me. They even helped me to purchase my own car, an old green Volkswagen making its way through its last year of existence. They were not, however, aware that my problems stemmed from a loss of faith in God, Christ, and the church. And at this time I was not prepared to reveal these things to them.

I continued working at the restaurant as a waiter and was doing quite well. On a Friday night I would easily make anywhere from seventy to a hundred dollars in tips. I opened up a savings and checking account and was gradually becoming self-sufficient in the world. My former superiors never gave me any financial assistance, nor did they ever contact me to see how I was doing.

On my free evenings I would visit some of the seminarians who were friends of mine. I must admit that there were times when I wished I was back with them, for their life was very comfortable and easy. But I knew that returning to the seminary would not work. I would not solve my problems by pretending to believe in a religion that now had no meaning for me. I began to realize that I would never return to what I once was. My energies were directed toward finding a place for myself in the world.

After I had been working at Emerson's for three months, John Radnay, the firm's president, approached me one evening and asked if I would be interested in becoming an assistant manager. I grabbed at the offer. Here was my opportunity for a professional job. I would be given a salary and benefits and more importantly a sense of security. I would again belong to an organization. I trained under Tony, was soon promoted to assistant manager, and was assigned to the steak house in Silver Springs, Maryland. I reported to the manager there on November 1, 1971 and began a career in the restaurant industry that was to last over twelve years.

Never would I or could I have imagined that my acceptance of this new opportunity would eventually lead to marriage, four children, and a conversion to God through the beautiful religion of Judaism.

✻ ✻ ✻ ✻ ✻ ✻

Human Love

Rabbis, priests, and ministers have always had a special place of importance and honor. For some reason we look upon them as being above the frailties of human nature. We expect and demand that their behavior be above reproach, and when one has the misfortune to fall, we feel angry and resentful. We are embarrassed by their show of frail humanity. How dare they be human!

Among Catholics these feelings are especially acute. The Catholic expects even more from his priest, not because priests are more intelligent, or even more pious, then other clergymen, but because of their vow of celibacy. Their voluntary acceptance of such an extraordinary life-style is the added dimension that causes many, even including non-Catholics, to pay them a special kind of deference.

For me a life of celibacy did not appear to be unreasonable. When I first decided to become a priest, I never gave thought to the fact that celibacy would be required and I would never be allowed to marry. It merely seemed like a way for a priest to have more time to minister to the needs of the people without being distracted by having to take care of a wife and family.

As a consequence of my celibacy, however, there were no personal relationships in my life. I shared my most intimate thoughts and feelings with Christ. My life was one of constantly working to intensify my relationship with Christ, and human relationships were not encouraged. Friendships between seminarians were monitored and almost always discouraged. We were not allowed to have a true friendship with any other person.

I suppose that this was intended to prevent any possibility of homosexual relationships developing, but in their zeal to protect us, our superiors stripped away part of our humanity. To this day I can honestly say that I find it very difficult to establish genuine friendships with other men. Imagine how much more difficult it was for me to form a friendship with someone of the opposite sex. There were women I met during my priesthood, some of them married, who had no evil intentions, but sought only to be good friends. Their friendships would have enhanced my humanity, but I would not allow them to know me or permit such a friendship. I kept all relationships on a superficial level. I received from them but would not reciprocate.

One married woman I especially remember, was a reporter for a local newspaper in Beverly, Massachusetts. She was an attractive woman, happily married to a fine man whom I also knew and met on many occasions. She phoned one day while I was still at the shrine in Ipswich to tell me she wanted to do a feature story on our youth programs. I agreed to cooperate, since the story would make the shrine and its programs all the more popular.

She had a very warm, outgoing personality, the kind that likes to touch and hold on to your arm. From the outset I felt ill at ease, seeing her as a threat to my celibacy and priesthood. When she completed the story, she personally delivered a copy of the text and then invited me to have lunch with her and her editor. I think she felt my reluctance, because she assured me that her husband would also be there. I accepted the invitation. Soon afterwards she called upon me at the shrine. She wanted to know more about what had motivated me to become a priest. I was so overly sensitive that it never dawned on me that reporters were naturally inquisitive, and I read something more personal into her questions. From time to time she would buy me a book and inscribe it with some brief thoughts about our friendship. I was afraid to reciprocate. I wasn't capable of sharing my feelings with others, male or female. Soon the friendship ended, and I never saw or heard from her again.

In defense of celibacy I would have to say, first, that it is possible to live and maintain this life-style. There are many priests who are faithful to their vow, but loneliness plays a large role in their lives. I especially would feel this during the Christmas holidays, when most families would be together, whereas I would be busy hearing confessions and celebrating mass at various churches in the area.

I remember one Christmas in particular that caused me to feel this loneliness. While stationed in Washington, I was scheduled to celebrate midnight mass at Andrews Air Force Base. I arrived there about eight in the evening, and, since I had not had dinner, entered the dining room. It was filled with servicemen and their families, all happily sharing this night with each other. I, on the other hand, was seated at the chaplain's table by myself. I can't recall ever having felt so alone. What made it so acute was that I was surrounded by families who were sharing the night with each other while I sat there by myself.

As students we had often been told of the sacrifice that celibacy would require of us. This was usually interpreted to mean abstinence from sex. That night, however, I experienced the deeper and more authentic meaning of the sacrifice of celibacy.

There were other experiences that taught me about the sacrifice that celibacy demanded. When my brother Michael was blessed with his firstborn, I went home to perform the rite of baptism—as a matter of fact, it was my first baptism as a priest. My brother, complaining about not being able to find a decent job, began teasing me about how good I had it as a priest.

Holding his baby in my arms, I replied, "Mike, you think I have such a great life, being a priest, not having to work and worry about money. You have everything right here. You have a son, a child, and that's something I will never have."

Often at weddings I would again be reminded of the sacrifice of the celibate. The right to have a bride that I too could love. Yes, celibacy can be lived, and as a priest I lived it and felt its demands. Nonetheless, as much as the joy at weddings appealed to me, I vowed that I would never leave the priesthood to marry. It was not the rigors of celibacy that made me leave the priesthood but my loss of faith.

To be quite honest, I sometimes feel that my many years as a celibate have left me emotionally crippled. As a priest I thought I knew what love was all about, but I soon discovered that it was not the kind of love upon which one could build human relationships. Celibate love is general and not directed to any one person or persons. I loved everyone—family, friends, even strangers—with almost the same degree of intensity. It was a love that wasn't messy and demanded nothing but time, of which I had plenty. At age thirty-two I was unprepared for human love. I avoided relationships with women and found no one for whom I would be willing to take the risk of entering a man-woman relationship.

Working in the restaurant offered me many social opportunities. I often found myself surrounded by women who, if only because of curiosity about my past, would have gone out with me. The feelings were never mutual. What free time I had, and it wasn't much, I usually spent with some of the seminarians with whom I still associated. On my free nights I would go out for dinner with them, usually at a fine Italian restaurant located in the marketplace. I felt comfortable with them. I found it easier to socialize with them than to go out with strangers. I was living in the world but certainly not fully a part of it.

I had been the assistant manager at the Silver Spring Emerson's for about a week. Before we opened the restaurant each day, I would hold a brief meeting with the lunch waitresses and give them any last-minute instructions. On this particular day I was sitting at a table with four of the waitresses, waiting for a new girl who had just started working there. While we were waiting, the conversation turned to my past life. They wanted to know if it was true that I had once been a priest. Yes, I was, I told them. Soon I was deluged with questions about religion.

The new girl finally arrived. She had beautiful black hair and large, warm brown eyes. She was different from the others, personable but at the same time aloof. I remember thinking to myself that this was the kind of girl I would like to know. I could envision her as my girlfriend.

She introduced herself as Diane and apologized for being late. I liked her. From that time on I made it a point to check the weekly schedule for her name and be sure that I was working on the days she was scheduled to work.

I was disappointed to discover that Diane only worked two or three days a week. She was attending Maryland University and, unlike the other girls, could not work full-time. Whenever she didn't come I would find myself down in the dumps. I never really talked to her, though, except on work-related matters, but I liked seeing her, and it was enough if she gave me a smile.

This secret "love affair" went on for several weeks. One day the bartender called me over. "Hey, John, do you like that girl?" pointing to Diane. "Yes," I said, "I wish I could take her out." Then, to my surprise, he said, "She thinks you're very nice."

Well, that was all I needed to hear. His remark bolstered my confidence enough to want to ask her out. The problem was how to approach her. The plan I devised would certainly today be regarded as a form of sexual harassment. At the end of lunch, the waitresses had to prepare the tables for dinner. Among other things, they had to wrap the silverware in napkins. As Diane was performing this task I came up to her and said, "Listen, if you'll go out to dinner with me tonight, you don't have to finish doing the silverware."

I said this in a joking manner, so that if she answered no I wouldn't be too embarrassed by the rejection. But Diane looked at me, smiled, and said, "Okay." Today she tells me that she only agreed in order to get out of doing the silverware, which she hated doing.

I couldn't believe she had said yes. I think I thanked her and then began to worry about where I would take her. Then I began to worry about the fact that my car was a beat-up old Volkswagen. How could I pick her up in such a heap? I wanted to impress her, I wanted her to like me. I thought of borrowing a better car, but since I didn't know anyone I could have asked, I had to take the chance and use the Beetle. Diane looked Italian, so I decided to take her to the Italian restaurant I frequented with the seminarians. It was a fancy place and the food was excellent.

After work I hurried over to the seminary to let some of my friends know that I had a date. I wanted them to be at the restaurant to see her. I guess I wanted to show her off. This kind of behavior probably seems childish. I imagine it's how normal guys behaved in high school or college. I was making up for lost time.

It was time to pick her up. There I was chugging down her street in my battered old car. She lived in College Park, which was not that far from my place, in an apartment she shared with three other girls. Diane answered as I knocked on the door. She was beautiful. I had never seen her in any other outfit except for her waitress uniform. My friends waiting at the restaurant would certainly be impressed. I guess she was doing the same thing, because all her room-mates were home that evening. She introduced me to them and I suppose received their opinions of me, because the three of them made a dash for one of the bedrooms with her just before we left.

Once in the car, which I apologized for, I began to feel a lot more comfortable. Diane has a way about her that makes you feel as if you've known her all your life. I asked her why she and her roommates had gone into the bedroom just before we left. She said they wanted to tell her that for an ex-priest I looked pretty handsome. Well, I guess she got their approval. Soon it would be my turn.

G & G's Restaurant was not in the safest or most exciting section of Washington, but, as is so often the case, the quality of food and service made up for the location. I could see that she was a bit apprehensive. I assured her that we were okay and that no one had ever been hurt or mugged coming to G & G's, at least not that I was aware of.

Once inside the restaurant we both felt better. "Oh," I said, in a voice indicating surprise, "look, some of the guys from the seminary are here. Let me introduce you to them." I took her over to their table and delighted in showing her off to them. Judging from the expressions on their faces, I could see that they approved.

That night I ordered my favorite items—clams casino for my appetizer, and steak pizzaola as entree. I wanted to order the same for Diane, but she insisted on having only a salad and rolls. I was kind of disappointed, since I had brought her to this place because of the good food. She told me that everything was fine but she simply was not hungry.

Our conversation centered on questions from Diane about the priesthood and why I had wanted to be a priest. I don't recall everything we discussed, but I do remember how good I felt being with her. Her personality was so warm and vivacious. I didn't want the evening to end.

When the waiter brought us the dessert menu, Diane again refused to have anything. I really felt bad, and she knew I was disappointed. "John," she said, "I have to tell you something, because I don't want you to think that I don't like the restaurant or the food it serves. I'm Jewish and I keep kosher."

"I don't care if you're Jewish," I replied, "but what is keeping kosher? Does it mean you can't eat meat?"

Diane then proceeded to explain the concept and religious meaning of keeping kosher. I not only found the explanation interesting but was surprised that a beautiful young woman would be so conscientious about the rules of her religion, especially in today's world. I had given up on religion, or maybe religion had given up on me, so I was all the more impressed.

I was the first Gentile Diane had ever dated, and she told me that she really shouldn't have accepted my invitation but had done so because she felt sorry for me and was curious about my having been a priest. She also said that I seemed like a nice person.

I didn't mind the questions about my past life, I replied, and the fact that she was Jewish didn't mean anything to me. What was important, I continued, was that I found her attractive and felt very comfortable with her. I wanted nothing else but to be friendly and maybe go out again, but this time to a movie. She didn't say yes, only that she would think about it. I drove her back to her place. I didn't want to say good night. I was beginning to miss her.

It was still early so I decided to stop in at the seminary and get the reviews from those who had been at the restaurant. Sadly, no one was home. I had no one to share this new and pleasant experience with that night. I drove back to my place thinking about my evening with Diane. I wondered if she would go out with me again. Well, even if she didn't, I would still be able to see her at work, and that would have to suffice.

The next day I told the bartender about my date with Diane and asked him to find out for me if she had enjoyed the evening. Later that day, as I was doing some paperwork in the office, I looked up her application and took down the phone number of her apartment and of her family in Balti-more. I found myself becoming more and more interested in her. I wanted to see her all the time. When she reported for work she told me she'd had a wonderful time and enjoyed my company.

This attraction to her was very exciting and at the same time scary. Exciting because for the first time in my life I truly felt something emotional, maybe love, for another person. Maybe love, because I wasn't sure what love for a girl was supposed to feel like. I loved my parents and family, but the feelings I had for them were not the same as those for Diane. Scary, though, because I found myself becoming less interested in my work. The hours required of me at the restaurant drastically reduced the amount of time I could spend with her.

More disconcerting, I discovered that I had feelings of jealousy. When Diane told me that she was dating other guys, I was angry and upset. And when she told me that they were dental and medical students, I felt that my brief relationship with her was over. I couldn't compete with them. They were Jewish, I wasn't. They had secure financial futures ahead of them, I did not. I was an ex-priest, assistant manager of a restaurant at $150 a week. I was very confused. I had never experienced so many contradictory feelings at the same time. Believe me, being celibate was a lot easier. Relationships were great, I was learning, but they sure caused a lot of pain.

It was now the end of December. Diane would be going home for the holidays. I called her at her apartment and asked if I could come over to talk. She agreed. Diane wouldn't hurt a soul, but when we met in her apartment she unknowingly almost devastated me. "Look, John," she said, "I like you, you're a nice guy, but we could never have a relationship that would grow. It's like we are from two different worlds."

I didn't want to hear what she was saying. I knew she was right.

She continued, "My parents would never allow me to see you, and if my sister Esther ever found out we went to dinner she would kill me." Esther, her only sister, and older than Diane, had no tolerance for Jews dating Gentiles. One can only imagine her reaction if she knew that I was even in Diane's apartment.

My first introduction to Esther was over the phone. While Diane was home during the Christmas holidays I found myself lost and lonely. I took the risk of calling her. The phone rang.

"Hello." The voice sounded just like Diane's so I said, "Hi, it's me, John."

"Who? Who are you?"

I quickly realized it was Esther. "Is Diane there?" I sheepishly asked.

"Yes she is. Who is this?"

"Tell her it's David Cohen."

I had not met Esther, but I could judge from our brief encounter on the phone what would be in store for me if I continued to see Diane.

When Diane got on, she again began to list reasons why we should not see each other anymore. None of them made any sense to me. So what if my brothers were construction workers, they made a decent living. They were good people. And the religious reasons she gave were equally upsetting. At that time I had no religion. I didn't care about God or any religion, I'd had enough of that. Now I found religion threatening to destroy a friendship that I wanted to develop. Diane admitted that she liked me and wished that the circumstances were favorable. We agreed to be friends but nothing more. I could see that it would never work out for us.

In spite of Diane's sometimes mean attempts to end our friendship, my fondness and admiration for her continued to grow. I began to realize that she felt some affection for me when she ended her vacation earlier than planned. That New Year's Eve I was working, since it was one of our busiest nights, and it was then that I knew she really cared about me.

Turning down a New Year's Eve date, Diane came with a friend to see me at the restaurant. When we closed I sat with her and her friend Barbara in one of the booths. I remember saying, "I think you're in love with me."

"What makes you think that," she asked.

"Well, if I were a beautiful girl like you, I would be out tonight, not sitting here with me drinking coffee." And then I said, "Diane, I think I love you. I know you don't want to hear that. I know we can never be together, but I at least wanted to let you know how I feel about you."

We were happy and unhappy at the same time. I wished the rest of the world would go away and leave us two alone.

Nothing ever seems to come easy for me. Normally boy meets girl, they fall in love, and they share their happiness with their families. Not for us, however. Neither of us was ready to tell our families. There was no reason to upset them. Maybe this relationship wouldn't last. We would wait for the right time. Meanwhile we saw each other more frequently.

I had never realized how much joy and pain a relationship could bring. When we were together I felt complete. When Diane left for Florida during the spring break, I felt as if part of me were missing. I was experiencing the fullness of a human relationship, and I didn't like the hurting side of it. Celibacy had produced its times of loneliness, but never had the pain been so great.

It dawned on me that I was really and truly in love with her. So this is what human love is all about, I mused, realizing that I had never fully comprehended the joy and pain of the many couples I thought I had helped as a priest. They had come to me for understanding and I had given them empty words. What else could I have done? Although I didn't know it at the time, a major part of my life had been empty.

The pain of separation finally gave way to joy when Diane returned. I had never thought I could miss someone so much. We both now realized that what we had never intended to happen had happened. Before us was an untraveled road. We could only guess what we would find along the way. The first stop had to be in Baltimore. There I would meet Diane's parents and for the first time enter a Jewish home. Human love, I was learning, was what really mattered in life, but like the life of celibacy, it too demanded sacrifices. But now these sacrifices would be shared by two.

$$* * * * * *$$

Shabbos Candles

*B*aruch *ata adonai elohainu melech ha-olam asher kidshanu b'mitzvotav v'tzivanu l'hadlik ner shel shabbat* ("Blessed art Thou, Lord our God, King of the universe, Who has sanctified us with His commandments and commanded us to kindle the Sabbath lights").

Sidney and Gertrude Max were long-time residents of Baltimore. Sidney, born in Poland, had come to America at the age of twenty-eight and had lived in Baltimore ever since. Tragically he had experienced the loss of his mother and sisters during the Holocaust. Gertrude had been born in Baltimore, where her father, Benjamin Gordon, was a prominent and well-respected businessman, and her mother, Lena, was a tireless worker for Hadassah and the *shul*. In due course Sidney and Gertrude met, courted, married, and were blessed with two daughters, Esther and Diane.

Like most parents, Sidney and Gertrude tried to provide the best for their children. They maintained an Orthodox home, sent both girls to Hebrew school, made sure that they were well instructed in the Jewish faith and hoped for the day when their daughters would bring home husbands who were not only observant but able to provide for them. To Jewish parents, the marriage of a daughter within the faith was a source of great joy, and their happiness would be greater still if the husband just happened to be a successful

111

doctor, dentist, or lawyer. So was the hope and wish of Sidney and Gertrude for their girls.

Esther, the eldest, had just gotten engaged to a law student, Howard Teller. Diane, feeling guilty about seeing me without her parents' knowledge, decided that this would be a good time to break the news to them. Since they were so happy about Esther, she reasoned, they would not be as upset when they learned about me.

It was while they were driving through downtown Baltimore that Diane broke the news to them. "Mom, Dad, I met a wonderful guy at work, he happens to be the assistant manager of the restaurant." Sidney and Gertrude looked at her in surprise. They could judge from Diane's voice that she was about to tell them something they didn't want to hear.

"He isn't Jewish," Diane quickly added.

Her mother's first response was, "Well, what's his name?"

Diane answered, "His name is John Scalamonti."

Trying to appear calm, Gertrude responded, "My, what a romantic-sounding name that is."

At that moment, Sidney turned to his wife and yelled, "What! Are you crazy?"

And that is all I know about the conversation between Diane and her parents. Maybe no one wants to tell me what was really said. How it came about that I was invited to their house for dinner no one seems to remember. Gertrude likes to play the psychologist: maybe she felt that if she treated this unexpected and unwanted development in a calm, nonthreatening manner, the whole thing would pass.

It's shocking enough for Jewish parents to have a daughter bring home a Gentile, but can you imagine not only a Gentile but a former priest? A man eight years older than their daughter, working as an assistant manager of a restaurant, and without a penny to his name. Wow, what a prize!

I'm sure that Sidney and Gertrude must have cried out to heaven, "Please, God, don't let this be! Put some sense into our daughter's head. Let this stranger go away! Amen and Amen!" They must have blamed each other. They must have wondered what awful deed they had done to deserve this. They must have told each other, "Maybe this infatuation of Diane's will pass. We'll be nice to him, welcome him to our home, and then say good-bye, forever."

I was full of fear and very nervous as I drove up to their house. At one point, on the way there, I decided to turn around and go back to my place. I would tell Diane that I had gotten lost. No, I'd go through with it. I pulled up in front of their house, walked over to the entrance, and haltingly pushed the door bell.

My thoughts raced one after another. What was I doing here? I had never before visited a Jewish home. There had never been any reason to do so. As a priest, I hadn't been in the habit of calling upon Jews. I knew the Jewish families in my hometown, I had even performed a marriage for a Jewish man and his Gentile bride. But I had never entered a Jewish home. Nor had I had the experience of calling upon the parents of a girl in order for them to meet the man who wanted to date their daughter. This was all so foreign to me.

Someone was coming to the door. It was Diane. She brought me into the den, and there, sitting on a sofa, were her parents, Sidney and Gertrude. Diane introduced me to them. They were both warm and gracious. They offered me a glass of wine, which I eagerly accepted, hoping it would calm my nerves.

I was very impressed with Sidney. He demonstrated a remarkable knowledge of the Catholic church and, for that matter, of other world religions. He was obviously well-read, and as I was to discover he had mastered seven languages, including Latin and Chinese. I liked him immediately.

Gertrude was beautiful and, I thought, very Italian-looking. She made me feel welcome, displaying a warm, friendly personality that told me at once that she was most certainly Diane's mother.

After some polite conversation we went into the dining room to enjoy a familiar meal of spaghetti and meatballs. What else would you serve an Italian to make him feel at home? I have always felt that this was a wonderful gesture on Gertrude's part. Diane and I have since wondered what subsequent events would have been like if Gertrude had served me gefilte fish on that first visit.

The Max home was warm and modern but somehow exhibited a sense of tradition. I had been in hundreds of Gentile homes, including the home of my parents, but I felt something different there. A certain indefinable something that told you you were in a Jewish home. Maybe it was the fact that the people living there were descendants of Abraham, who had lived more than five thousand years before them. Maybe it was because this was a home in which religious rituals were performed and Shabbos was observed. I have since tried to define what I felt, but somehow cannot express it in concrete terms. Other Jews I have spoken to tell me they understand what I mean but likewise cannot define it in words.

In any case, I began to feel comfortable. I liked it there and I liked Diane's parents. The conversation at table centered mostly upon my past life as a priest. I'm sure they were hoping there would be no future life to discuss, at least no future life that would include Diane. Gertrude was very concerned about how my mother had taken the news of my leaving the priesthood. I could see that she was a very compassionate and sensitive person. I would see this same compassion on behalf of my mother when I declared my intention of converting to Judaism.

As this indicated, Gertrude was always more concerned about the welfare of others than about herself. I once remarked to Diane, "Your mother would be considered an ideal Christian by the Catholic church. She is more Christian than many of the Christians I knew as a priest."

On the one hand, I was paying Gertrude a compliment,

but at the same time I was expressing the belief held by many Christians that Jews are not charitable people. In all honesty, I was surprised to find a Jew so charitable and so "other-centered." I was surprised to discover that Gertrude was the "Good Samaritan" of the Christian Bible. On many occasions, while driving in downtown Baltimore, she would stop her car to help a stranger in need. I doubt that I or many of my priestly friends would have done the same.

Throughout my Christian and priestly life I had been taught that Christians were different from everyone else because they lived by Christ's law of love. Christ was the model to be followed, "Greater love hath no man than this, that he lay down his life for his friends" (John 15:13). Such an act would be considered the zenith of a Christian's life.

In contrast, Jews, so I was taught, believed and lived by the laws of the so-called Old Testament, which were summed up in the famous phrase, "eye for eye, tooth for tooth" (Exodus 21:24). Some Christian literature reduces the teachings of Judaism to a simple adherence to the 613 commandments. They view Judaism as a religion of law that fosters legalism and promises salvation to those who follow the rules most strictly, a religion whose teachers are concerned about the letter of the law, and not about its spirit.

Sadly, because of ignorance and prejudice, many Christians subscribe to these mistaken notions. My teachers had insisted that it was impossible to lead a life guided by love without the help of Christ. I was confused. How could Gertrude, then, be such a woman? She had never known Christ, she had never received the sacraments. What made it possible for her to lead such a charitable and "Christian" life?

Imagine my surprise when I discovered that it was Hillel, who lived a century earlier, and not Christ, who first taught the golden rule. "Do not do unto others what you would not want others to do unto you," he said, "The rest is commentary, go and study it" (Shabbat 31a).

Similarly, due to ignorance of Judaism, I once believed Christ's statement, "By this shall all men know that you are my disciples, if you have love one for another," to be original. But Jewish sages long before him always taught that the three characteristics which set the Jew apart from the heathen were mercy, modesty, and kindness, and that it was by the living of these virtues that the Chosen of God were recognized.

I found Judaism to be a religion of love and kindness because I had the good fortune of meeting two Jews who by their words and actions showed me that they were "of a good heart," and lived the virtues their religion taught. I refer lovingly to my in-laws, Sidney and Gertrude Max. In their home were the seeds of Judaism sown in my heart.

Other than the fact that I was a Gentile, I do not think they found any great fault in me, for I was soon invited to attend Shabbos dinner on Friday night. I brought along a bottle of unkosher wine, obviously not knowing any better, and they didn't make me feel embarrassed because of it. The smell of chicken soup and other good foods captured my attention as I walked in the door. The house was immaculately clean. The dining room table was covered with a white linen tablecloth. On the table were two brass candlesticks which quite resembled those used on the altar when I said mass. There was an atmosphere of expectation. I could not imagine why coming to dinner this time seemed so different.

Sidney wasn't home, he was at shul. Diane was busy helping her mother in the kitchen, so I sat in the den and watched television. Soon I heard Diane's mom call her. "Diane tell John to turn off the television and come and light candles."

Diane came in and said, "You have to turn off the television now, my mother and I have to light our candles."

"Oh, okay," was my intelligent response. I had no idea what lighting candles meant. There was a large mirror on the wall in the den, and in it I could see a reflection of the dining room table. Soon Gertrude appeared before the table. She placed two candles in the holders and then proceeded to perform a ritual I had never seen or heard of. As I watched, she lit the candles and then began to motion her hands over them. Then she covered her face with her hands and appeared to be praying.

When she finished she walked over to Diane, kissed her, and said, "Good Shabbos." Then she came into the den, kissed me on the cheek, and said, "Good Shabbos." I think I may have answered with "Thank you." Diane followed her into the room, also kissed me, and said, "Good Shabbos, John."

The scent of the burning candles reminded me of the services in a church. "Why were you and your mother lighting candles?" Diane began to explain the ritual to me. I thought, what a beautiful ceremony. What was most impressive was the fact that this ritual took place in the home and was performed by women. The only rituals I knew were performed in the church; the mass I had once said in my home had been a very special exception.

The idea of welcoming Shabbos in such a manner gave me a feeling of warmth and piety that I had not experienced for some time. Today, because of God's grace, I see my wife and two eldest daughters perform this beautiful ritual in our home every Friday night. Often it brings back the memory of that first candle-lighting ceremony I observed almost twenty years ago.

Soon Sidney came home. I can hear him now, "Good Shabbos, Good Shabbos," he said as he came through the door and into the house. And then, as he did every week without fail, he went over to his wife and Diane and kissed them as he greeted them with the now familiar, "Good Shabbos." Next he came over to me, shook my hand, and greeted me with, "Good Shabbos, John." Sidney and I sat together in the living room while Diane and her mother prepared the table. When I told him my thoughts on the candle-lighting ritual, he began to explain, in more detail, about its origins and how sacred a tradition it was amongst observant Jews. The two candles, he said, represent the two expressions of the fourth commandment: remembering to keep the Sabbath holy and observing the Sabbath. The women of the house are given priority in performing this ritual, but if no women are present the man may light the candles.

I listened with interest to Sidney's explanation of the rites and symbols of Judaism. As we were talking, Diane looked in and announced that dinner was ready. "Wait, let me get the wine I brought." Sidney looked at it and laughed, "I know you meant well, John, but this wine isn't kosher, we can't use it." I could see that he didn't want to hurt my feelings by not accepting it. I felt sorry that I had brought an unkosher product into their home.

The Shabbos table looked great, and the food looked and smelled terrific. But what really caught my attention was a silver chalice filled with wine; it resembled one I had used at mass, but was much smaller. Then I saw, at Sidney's place, two loaves of bread covered with a white cloth. The symbols of bread and wine were so familiar to me. I had used bread and wine when saying mass. I could not help but think how much the table in front of me, with its white cloth, the lit candles, the cup of wine, and the bread, looked like the altar upon which I had said mass.

How similar and yet, as I would find, how very different. The Jewish wine symbolized joy, the Catholic wine, the blood shed by Christ. The Jewish bread symbolized the staff of life, the manna which sustained the Chosen in the desert. The Catholic bread symbolized the broken body of a man. The meal at the Jewish table was a festive, joyous family occasion. The mass at the Catholic table, a remembrance of the sacrifice and death of a god-man. Both tables were set for religious experiences, both used the same symbols, but each expressed a totally different meaning.

I could not help but make these associations in my mind. I would find many other such similarities during my journey into Judaism. Before we began the meal, for instance, Sidney gave me a *yarmulke* to wear. A similar head covering is worn by the popes and bishops of the Catholic Church. It is referred to in the liturgy as the *soli Deo*, which means, [removed] "only for God."

Or to give another example: on occasions when the name of Jesus is pronounced or after the consecration of the bread and wine, it is believed that God's presence is on the altar. I thought of this when I watched Sidney raise the cup of wine and in Hebrew say the special Shabbos blessing, "Blessed art Thou, Lord our God, King of the universe, Who creates the fruit of the vine." And then the blessing over the bread, "Blessed art Thou, Lord our God, King of the universe, Who brings forth bread from the earth." These were the same words I had pronounced over the wine and bread during the celebration of the mass. The difference here was that the Shabbos meal was taking place in the sanctity of a Jewish home and not in a church on a cold, marble altar. Here the father of the family performed the role of priest and leader. Here was an act of religion and faith performed as part of a festive meal, shared with family and loved ones. For me this first Shabbos dinner was a welcoming experience, one that left me eager to share in it again.

But of all the Jewish holidays and rituals I found the Passover Seder to be the most moving. I had some vague knowledge about the Seder meal because Catholic theology describes the Last Supper as having been a Seder. But I had learned about the Passover ritual only as historical background for the origin of the Catholic sacraments of holy orders and the eucharist, both of which are thought to have been established by Christ at the Last Supper.

When Diane and her parents invited me to their Seder, I accepted eagerly. I again brought a bottle of wine, but this time I made sure it was kosher. Later I discovered that it wasn't kosher for Passover. Hard to keep up. The bottle was left outside and later that evening returned with me to my apartment.

My first Passover Seder was a powerful educational experience. The reading of the *Haggadah*, which I followed in English, made me realize who the Jewish people are and what they are all about. Here I was, a Gentile, commemorating with Jews the deliverance of the children of Israel from over two centuries of Egyptian slavery. Here I was a Gentile, being brought back in time through the Passover rituals to witness the exodus from Egypt almost four thousand years ago. On this night we celebrated the freedom of the Jewish people and the beginning of the journey that would finally lead to the Promised Land. I saw and experienced through the Seder the history of the Chosen People of God. The rituals and symbols, so rich in meaning, began to arouse in me a desire to learn more about these Chosen People and their God, but I kept this to myself until such time as I believed I was truly prepared to take the first step of a journey that would lead me to become one of His Chosen.

At the Seder I finally met Diane's sister Esther and her fiancé, Howard. Esther's feelings about dating Gentiles were well-known to her family. She was against it and said so in no uncertain terms. I could understand her disapproval. She was then and is now a good sister to Diane, and she was looking out for what she saw as Diane's best interests. Esther was kind and respectful toward me that night, but her message was loud and clear: if I really loved Diane, I would not come to see her again. I would do what was best for everyone, and that would be to end the relationship. I could not find fault with Esther's attitude. I understood that her relationship with Howard was made easy and natural by their sharing the same religious beliefs and culture. Maybe it would be best to follow her advice.

Sharing in Shabbos dinner and the Passover Seder aroused a desire to seek out the source from which these rituals and symbols derived. The smell of burning wax from the candles reminded me of the spiritual life I had once possessed and now longed to have again. The taste of Shabbos wine and the eating of blessed hallah had become as spiritual food for my impoverished soul.

✳ ✳ ✳ ✳ ✳ ✳

Why Judaism?

Why become a Jew? I am asked that question by almost everyone I meet, Gentile and Jew alike. The Gentiles ask because they cannot fathom how a former priest of the Catholic church could accept a religion that does not recognize Jesus as God and Messiah. "How could you turn your back on Jesus?" Some have even called me a Judas, linking me with the apostle who according to the Christian Bible betrayed Christ. Others believe that I became a member of the Jewish people only to be able to marry Diane.

I have no difficulty when a Christian asks me why I became a Jew; I am, however, confused as to why a born Jew would ask it. Sometimes I get the feeling that a Jew who asks this really believes, deep down, that there is something wrong with being a Jew. A Jew who finds it hard to understand why I would give up shrimp and lobster, or why I keep kosher when he gave it up after his mother died is obviously someone who does not appreciate the Jewish religion. Such people are often nonobservant and make no place in their homes and lives for the ancient rites and symbols that Judaism has to offer them.

I often try to explain to such people why I find Judaism so attractive and fulfilling. Too often born Jews apologize for their religion and for the actions of their fellow Jews. They are ashamed to say that they are members of the Chosen People. How great is my hope that upon reading my story

122

they will be moved to return to the Judaism I have come to know and love.

Who would have imagined that my witnessing of the lighting of Shabbos candles would open my mind and heart to a religion I had once believed to be false? There is no doubt that the light from those candles inspired me to set out on a course which has still not reached its end. Sharing in a Shabbos dinner stirred in me a hunger to learn and to know. The more questions I raise about Judaism, the more I am drawn into it, whereas the more I questioned my Christian faith, the more I found myself doubting it.

For me, one of the most appealing aspects of Judaism is the importance it gives to the home and to the practice of religious rites in the home. It may seem that I overemphasize this aspect of Judaism, but understand that for me, considering who and what I was, this element of Judaism is the cornerstone upon which I have continued to build the rest of my Jewish life. As a priest I was always moved by the church's liturgical rites and symbols, but the sacred rites of Catholicism could only be performed by a priest within the confines of a sanctuary—the church. In Judaism, the home itself is a sanctuary, and in it the father, acting, as it were, as a priest, performs a whole series of beautiful rituals and prayers with and for his family.

In my eyes, the eight-day observance of Passover, with its laws of *hametz* and *matzah* and the elaborate Seder, forcefully emphasizes the teaching that the Jewish home is a sanctuary and the source from which our religious life is nourished. How different from Catholicism, where the observance of holidays was relegated to mass at the parish church, and there were no special rituals in the home, except for having a tree during the Christmas season, and I doubt that many regarded this practice as a religious ritual.

I have always had a positive attitude, one that looks at a glass and sees it as half full rather than half empty. Judaism,

I discovered, is a religion of optimism, "God saw all that He had made, and found it very good" (Genesis 1:31).

This too I found profoundly appealing. Judaism views the world as good, unlike Christianity, which sees it as a threat to achieving eternal salvation. For the Jew the world is a beautiful place, no doubt far from perfect, but designed by the hand of God, and offering many opportunities for love, family, and friendship. Judaism teaches us to love the world and to use its many gifts in a responsible manner, thereby making the world a more perfect and holier place in which to live.

Unlike Christianity, which demands that one reject the world in order to attain holiness, Judaism teaches that it is by living in the world, in accordance with the teachings of Torah, that the individual not only becomes holy himself but sanctifies the world. By living his daily life in this world according to the teachings and instructions of the Torah, the Jew finds salvation within himself. Thus there is no need in Judaism for a "god made man" to bring salvation.

One has only to read history to see that because of Judaism the world has become a more perfect and holy place. Through its teachings on life and the right to individual freedom, Judaism has done more good for the world than any other religion or philosophy. And considering our small numbers, Judaism has surpassed all other religions in producing individuals who have made major contributions in such fields as medicine, science, and education. Much more needs to be done, and herein lies the mission of the modern Jew: to continue to preserve life in all its forms, and to cherish and live each moment of life according to God's plan.

For one whose early life was spent in rejecting the normal and natural needs of his body, the teachings of Judaism on how to view and accept our bodies was indeed attractive. Catholicism, influenced by the teachings of Paul, regards the body as a stumbling block and a prison. The more one punishes and denies the body, the greater his reward in heaven. Earthly pleasures are to be shunned at all costs. Suffering and pain are good for the soul. Virginity and celibacy are the highest form of life on earth. Thus the highest ideals of the Christian life can be attained only by those who lead a supernatural existence, removing themselves from the world, consecrating themselves through sacred vows of poverty, chastity, and obedience. Ordinary people like my family might be good but could never attain the heights of holiness, whereas the priest—and so I believed about myself at the time—lives on a much higher plane. How often lay-people used to say to me, "Father, I wish I could be as holy as you, I wish I could live a life that would bring me closer to God."

How different in Judaism. "You shall be to Me a kingdom of priests, a holy nation" (Exodus 19:6). In Judaism religion and life are one and the same. There is no teaching or talk of living a supernatural life. There are no levels of holiness to which some are called and others not. At birth we are all blessed with life. The life God gives us is pure and good, and Judaism teaches us how to live it in such a way that we can sanctify the gifts of creation. The Torah does not call on us to reject the world or to renounce what God has called good in order to become a holy nation, a holy people. All are called to be holy, whether married or unmarried, educated or uneducated, rich or poor.

In Judaism, I found, holiness and sanctification exist in marriage, for husband and wife united together bring holiness into the home. The laws of the Torah and the Talmud do not separate man from his home or his work or the world in which he lives. Rather, they connect us with God no matter where we are and no matter what we are doing.

Observing the ethical laws sanctifies our daily work and our dealings with others. Enjoying the rest of Shabbos sanctifies the day and those who observe it. Eating kosher food sanctifies a common meal. Our meals become special because the food we place on our tables is God's food—food that nourishes the spirit as well as the body, because adhering to the dietary laws means that we are conscious of God even in the midst of so ordinary an act as eating.

Judaism teaches us to attain holiness by living in the image of God, as told to us in the sacred Scriptures: "You shall be holy, for I, the Lord your God, am holy" (Leviticus 19:2). The more we imitate His qualities of love, kindness, forgiveness, and faithfulness in our everyday human lives, the more holy we become and the more we fulfill our mission of sanctifying the world. How different a teaching from what I knew as a boy and a priest. How simple yet profound a teaching. A teaching that allows one to remain fully human, to love one's human life, yet to become holy and cause the world to become holy.

Nothing points out more clearly the gap between the Jewish and Catholic views of the world and life than the Catholic doctrine of original sin. Judaism sees the birth of a child as a great *simcha*, a gift from God Himself. The Christian, too, rejoices at the birth of a child, but sees the baby as born with original sin on its soul. This means that the infant is in a state of serious sin which has been transmitted by our first parents, Adam and Eve, and if it should die before baptism is administered, its soul will not be allowed entry into heaven. How harsh and pessimistic a view of the beginning of human life. How different the teachings of Judaism, which denies any such a state as original sin.

In short, Christianity focuses on the life to come, while Judaism is primarily concerned with how we live here and now, knowing that according to the Talmud, "The righteous of all nations will share in the world-to-come" (Tosefta, Sanhedrin 13:2). This emphasis on life—on the sacredness of life and the beauty of creation, including our bodies— found a recipient soul in me. Without knowing it, I had been longing for a religion that would enable me to unite mind and heart and totally worship God. In Judaism's teaching that one becomes fully human and holy by living the Torah, I discovered a oneness which in its own way reflects the nature of the One God from Whom all life has its beginning.

"Hear, O Israel, the Lord our God, the Lord is One." Not very long ago I watched a Catholic religious program called "Mother Angelica, Live." During the program a priest delivered a short sermon on how one can develop a personal relationship with God. The method he suggested was this: First go to Jesus and ask him to go and introduce you to his father. If for some reason you cannot approach Jesus, then go to his mother, Mary, and ask her to introduce you to her son, who then will introduce you to his father. If for some reason you cannot go to Mary, then go to a favorite saint and ask him (or her) to introduce you to Mary, who then will introduce you to Jesus, who then will introduce you to the father. This method of approaching God may seem almost humorous, but it is, in summary form, the Catholic teaching on prayer and the methods one can use to approach God. In Judaism, however, God requires no intermediaries. He is my personal God.

The purpose of religion, I believe, is to help us, as individuals, to establish a personal relationship with God. A religion that fails in this regard is not fulfilling its obligation to its adherents. The relationship we seek with God should be no less than the relationship between a husband and his wife. It should be a relationship marked by mutual love and respect, with no one else needed as intermediary or messenger.

Christianity maintains that "no one comes to the father except through the son" (John 6:65). But in Judaism I found a religion whose message speaks of One God, Who is my Father and Who hears my prayers without the voice of another. He is revealed to me in the Torah, and He speaks directly to me. In Judaism all God's children are equal. There are no classes that can claim they are closer to Him or that He only speaks to them. We are all "a kingdom of priests and a holy nation" (Exodus 19:6). In Judaism I found a religion that encourages me to seek God and to establish with Him a relationship that mirrors the one between Him and Israel. Long ago the prophets exhorted the people of Israel to be to God as a bride is to her groom. Today their words still call to His People to live the sacred covenant, to be faithful to their relationship and to grow in it.

Because of Judaism I was able to find God again. Most convincing to me that He exists is the Torah's teaching about the promises made to Abraham over four thousand years ago. "I will make you a great nation, and I will bless you. All the families of the earth shall bless themselves by you" (Genesis 12:2–3). Today the descendants of Abraham are one of the important peoples of the world. Other civilizations that were stronger and more numerous no longer exist, but Judaism does. Today we have our own state, the State of Israel, in what was once the promised land of Canaan. The One God made promises to Abraham; today we see those promises fulfilled. Judaism reveals the One God; the Torah reveals the one plan for this world, the one standard of right and wrong. "Hear, O Israel, the Lord our God, the Lord is One." How refreshing and uncomplicated it had become for me to pray again.

Speaking of complications, Catholicism is replete with doctrines and dogmas—articles of faith that must be unquestioningly accepted and believed. To add insult to injury, none of these doctrines has any practical implications for the here and now. A Catholic is continually told, "Live your religion, live your faith." But other than following the Ten Commandments, how can one live by the trinity, the immaculate conception, papal infallibility, the assumption? How do you translate a set of theological beliefs into the actions of everyday life?

Judaism, on the other hand, offers a daily way of life that can be lived here and now. Even the principles of faith set down by Maimonides are regarded not as infallible dogmas that a Jew must accept under pain of sin, but as guidelines, or perhaps even as no more than one outstanding Jew's view of the essence of the Jewish faith.

The Torah is filled with information about the existence of God. It tells us about the creation of the universe, God's great love for the people of Israel, the covenant between God and Israel, and similar topics. The Talmud is filled with discussions and differing opinions about the nature and attributes of God and other matters of faith, but no set of dogmas or creeds is imposed on us. Judaism tells me how to live, it provides me with a code of behavior that requires me to treat all men equally, honestly, and without prejudice. It offers me and my family a way of life which encourages us to enjoy the gifts of this world while at the same time making them holy.

As a Jew I know what it means to live my religion. I know that a Jew must be kind and forgiving, compassionate and understanding toward others. I know that as a Jew my life must display modesty, kindness, and mercy. For the Christian it is enough to say, "I believe." The Jew must live what he believes. I have often heard Gentiles claim that Jews are unforgiving and uncharitable, that they follow the laws of a harsh, unforgiving "Old Testament God." How wrong this is. The Torah is filled with examples and teachings of God's love and forgiveness.

What really brought this home to me was the difference between charity and *tzedakah* (the Hebrew term for giving to others).

The word *charity* comes from the Latin *caritas*, meaning "love." In Christianity charity is a virtue of surpassing kindness, something one does as an expression and reflection of his inner goodness. By contrast, the Hebrew word *tzedakah* means "righteousness," and it is because it is the right thing to do that a Jew gives to others.

At first glance the Jewish approach may seem cold and unfeeling. But consider, you do an act of charity because it makes you feel good. At any given moment, depending on whether or not you are in a charitable mood and how you feel toward the person in need, you are free to give or not give. A Jew, however, gives because it is his obligation as a decent human being to do so. His own feelings don't matter—the feelings of the poor person do.

This difference is implicit in the Torah's teaching regarding the harvest. The farmers may not harvest the corners of their fields, and the grain there is left for the poor to gather for their own use. This is not done out of kindness, but because the leftover grain belongs to the poor by right and they should not have to beg for it. Thus the Torah protects the lives and also the self-respect of the poor.

In all of my education at the seminary, no such teaching was ever given to me. Protecting the feelings of others is so important in Judaism that "spilling another's blood" is the talmudic idiom for embarrassing someone. A story about this dating from long before the time of Christ shows that Judaism has always taught its children to love one another and be kind to the stranger.

There once was a very observant Jew who kept all the statutes to the letter of the law. One day he met a rabbi and invited him to Shabbos dinner. The man told his wife to make sure the house was extra clean, the food especially good, and the Shabbos table set properly.

When the rabbi arrived, everything looked perfect, but as the man began the blessing over the wine, he noticed that his wife had forgotten to cover the hallah. Very angry, he snapped at her, "You stupid woman, how could you forget to cover the hallah?"

Suddenly, the rabbi got up and headed for the door. "Rabbi," the man called, "Where are you going?"

The rabbi answered, "I cannot remain in your house or eat at your table, this Shabbos meal is *tref*" [nonkosher].

"No," said the man, "I assure you that all my food is kosher."

The rabbi turned and said, "Because of the way you insulted and embarrassed your wife in my presence, your table is *tref* and I cannot partake of your meal."

The message is that although rituals are important in Judaism, they are not its essence. Embarrassing his wife was a sin and made the other Shabbos rituals unacceptable to God.

Kindness and respect for others is a central teaching of Judaism and the Torah. Judaism teaches respect for all people of all faiths. It does not criticize other faiths, especially those that believe in the One, True God. There is no room for prejudice in the heart of a practicing Jew.

The fact that the Jewish people are the Chosen People has in no way made the descendants of Abraham boastful or arrogant. If anything, I have discovered, most Jews are uncomfortable with this designation. Judaism teaches that we Jews are the Chosen not because we are superior to others, but because God has selected us to fulfill the dictates of His covenant. Through us the world has come to know the One, True God, and through us the world has become, and will become, a better and holier place.

What a shame that Judaism was presented to me, at the seminary, as a religion whose time had ended with the advent of Christ. We were taught that it had served its purpose because Christ had brought it to its completion. A "new covenant" had been issued, a new chosen people formed, a new Bible had come into being, called the "New Testament," and the sacred Torah, from which Jesus taught, was now called the "Old Testament."

I believed all this without, of course, ever having studied the Torah or the Talmud. I assumed that Judaism had nothing to offer—with one exception, the Ten Commandments. How ashamed I am today. For as I have discovered, and continue to discover, the sacred teachings of Judaism contain all that man needs to establish a new Garden of Eden.

As a Jew I know what it means to "live your religion." By

living my Judaism I love God, and in loving God I love my neighbor, so fulfilling what even Jesus acknowledged to be the greatest commandments, "Love the Lord, your God" (Deuteronomy 6:5) and "love your neighbor as yourself" (Leviticus 19:18). In the teachings of Judaism I have found a place where the spiritual and the material are one and not distinct, where everyday life and its activities are sanctified.

Little wonder that I was so eager to learn more about this religion. What very little I have written here and the few teachings I had learned were enough to make me want to become a part of so great a people with so great a message to offer the world. I sought then on my own to find a way which would grant me admittance into the Chosen People of God.

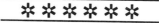

My Conversion

My conversion to Judaism seems to set many people, especially Jews, on edge. At the end of one of my talks, for instance, a woman asked, "If Diane and her parents had been Buddhists, would you have converted to Buddhism?" It seems like a reasonable question, since I never displayed any interest in Judaism before I met Diane and her family, but in asking it she is really saying that to her mind no one would accept Judaism unless he had an ulterior motive.

Many others seem to think I gave up Catholicism to get married or to taste a few luxuries. "I'll be blunt in responding. The priesthood was too good a life to be given up simply for a woman. Nor was celibacy, no matter how difficult at times, reason enough to leave the priesthood or my faith. If celibacy were my reason, I could have remained a Christian and entered the Protestant ministry, which allows for a married clergy.

Would that it had been so simple! It may well be that Diane and her family were the catalysts that helped work a transformation in my spiritual life, but they only had this effect because of what my inner development had been to that point. A Buddhist catalyst would not have affected me.

Whatever the ultimate reason, I had lost the gift of faith that had once inspired me to become a priest. Not only did I lose my faith in the church and in Christ, but I found myself questioning the very existence of God. When I met Diane I

133

was in a state of spiritual darkness. I'd had enough of religion and thought I had given up my quest.

For these reasons, my acceptance of Judaism was not a matter of convenience. It was a rediscovery of the One, True God, a God I had once believed in and then had lost. For this reason, I think, it is best described by the Hebrew word *teshuvah*, "returning," for it was my return to God. And this "return" was accompanied by much suffering and hardship. And the journey upon which I have embarked is only just beginning.

You can't imagine the expressions on the faces of Sidney and Gertrude when I told them that I wanted to learn about Judaism. I thought they would be pleased. Instead, I met resistance and discouragement.

Gertrude I know, was very upset. Not because she thought it wrong for me to study Judaism but because she believed it would break my mother's heart. She was always concerned about other people, and she knew how sad she would be if one of her children decided to become a Christian.

Sidney's response was more pragmatic. "If people know that you're a Jew, they'll give you a difficult time at work. Some won't even hire you. Why become a member of a religion that has always been persecuted and despised?"

Even Diane did not encourage me. "Don't do it for me," she said, "I would never ask you to do such a thing."

I had thought everyone would be happy to hear of my decision. But they weren't. Maybe Gertrude and Sidney feared that my converting would bring Diane and me closer to marriage, because I certainly wasn't their choice for her. We had been seeing each other, but so far we had never considered getting engaged.

Somehow I had to convince the three of them that my interest in Judaism was honest and sincere. I said I would like to see a rabbi, and it was decided that I should talk with Rabbi Max, Sidney's cousin. When Gertrude called and told him the story, he was, to say the least, very upset that they had even let me into their home. No, he would not meet with me, and he strongly suggested that they throw me out at once and make sure that Diane never saw me again.

Ironically, his attitude turned out to be helpful. Gertrude and Sidney were upset about the way he had spoken to them and embarrassed by his refusal to even talk to me. They may have hoped that he would get them off the hook by turning me away, but now, it seemed, they were willing to help me find another rabbi who might be more forbearing.

Someone suggested Rabbi Samuel Rosenblatt, the son of Cantor Yossel Rosenblatt. He too was an Orthodox rabbi, but he did not know the family. When I called to make an appointment he was quite gracious and courteous. In person he turned out to be a warm, personable elderly man who looked just as I imagined a rabbi ought to look. I felt comfortable in his presence.

Rabbi Rosenblatt listened respectfully when I recounted my story and told him of my deep interest in Judaism. He asked if my family was aware of my intentions. No, I said, and they would probably be very upset. He told me to go home and carefully consider the consequences of my actions, and if I was still interested, I was to call him.

I went back to Diane's late that afternoon and found them in the kitchen eating dinner. "Well, how did it go?" Sidney asked. "The rabbi liked me," I blurted out. "He said to give it serious thought, and if I was still interested to call him."

Judging by their slow, almost hesitant reactions, I could see that they didn't share my enthusiasm.

"He thinks you should convert?" Sidney asked.

"No, he didn't say that. He said I should call him if I seriously want to learn about Judaism."

"So what are you going to do?" asked Gertrude.

I told her that I wanted to study Judaism with Rabbi Rosenblatt. He felt that my motives were sincere and honest, and therefore that it was possible for me to convert, I said, and that was just what I had needed to hear from someone like him. I was determined to go ahead, I added, whether they approved or not. In a few days I would call him back and let him know of my intentions to become a Jew.

Soon I became a student of the rabbi's. We met each week, and I looked forward to seeing him each time. His instruction was fascinating, although I would have understood more and better if I had been versed in Hebrew at that point in my life. My knowledge of the Scriptures was more than adequate, however, and I probably had a better background in Bible study than most born Jews. I was also familiar with early Jewish history both as revealed in the Scriptures and from secular sources. Our course of study gave a lot of time to the ritual practices of Judaism, and also to the holidays and festivals. In addition there was much that I had to read on my own, and afterwards he would question me on the assignments.

The weeks of instruction quickly turned into months, and soon I was preparing myself to appear before the *beth din*. In accordance with Jewish law, the three members of this rabbinic tribunal questioned me on some of the weightier commandments and some of the lesser ones, to ascertain my grasp of what being Jewish entailed.

The rituals of conversion were to be administered in two stages. The first involved the rite of circumcision, the sign of the covenant. The second was an immersion in the mikvah.

Although I had been medically circumcised as an infant, it was still necessary for the religious rite to be performed in a modified form, albeit one that would cause blood to be drawn. I would be lying if I said that I looked forward to this. Before I began my instruction with Rabbi Rosenblatt I had assumed that another circumcision would not be needed. The rabbi, however, made me painfully aware that this would not be the case.

And so, in the presence of three rabbis, the ancient rite was now performed upon me, establishing the ancient covenant again between God and His creature soon to be counted as one of His Chosen People. Would that at the moment of this rite my thoughts had been focused on the religious significance of what was taking place. I found myself too distracted by what I hoped were the skillful hands of the *mohel*. Only after he had completed his task successfully did I begin to appreciate the gift I had received.

Although the conversion would not be complete until my immersion in the waters of the mikvah, I felt that I was now a part of the Jewish people. A week later, on August 13, 1972, I went to the mikvah and in the presence of three rabbis underwent the ritual bath required of all converts to the Jewish faith. The experience of the mikvah was spiritually renewing. It was as if the waters removed my old self and at the same time brought forth a new being. I was now truly entering the House of Israel as a new person, and to signalize this I had a new name, Johanan David a son of our father Abraham. It was the third day of Elul in the year 5732.

The intensity of my emotions on that day cannot be felt now, but the memory of the experience survives. I was filled with pride to have been accepted into the House of Israel. I rushed over to Diane's house, eager to tell her and her family about the experience I had just undergone. I felt a great sense of unity with them, knowing that I would now share in the heritage that was theirs. I guess my response to Gertrude's question summed it up in one word. "Well, how does it feel to be a Jew," Gertie asked. And I responded, "Great!"

It has been twenty years since that day in August of 1972. I can say that it was truly a new beginning, a new life for me. I found myself then at the beginning of a journey, one which sees no end. I only know that since the time of my conversion I have become more of a Jew, and the more I know of Judaism the more convinced I am that my place is truly in the House of Israel.

I am often asked whether it was very difficult for me to accept and practice Judaism. The answer always is yes and

no. It was never difficult for me to accept the teachings of
the Jewish faith, the essence of Judaism. What was difficult
were the many requirements imposed by the dietary laws
and the other elements of the halakhah. Even the simple act
of opening a *siddur* and learning to read from right to left
was difficult at first. How many times would I find myself
picking up the siddur in shul and automatically opening it
up to the back pages. And how often did I look with envy
upon those men whose davening reminded me of the beautiful movements of ballerinas, while my feeble efforts
brought back memories of my first attempt to learn dancing
while in grammar school, ugly and awkward. And it's a pity,
that I never videotaped my first attempt at putting on tefillin.
What a tangle of straps and boxes!

Becoming familiar with the many requirements of Jewish
ceremonial law was difficult but certainly not impossible.
The demands for fasting in Catholicism were minuscule as
compared to the fast of Yom Kippur. When I learned that as
a Jew you must fast, I didn't think much of it. I assumed that
it would be not unlike what had been demanded in my
former religion. On Catholic fast-days one is allowed to eat
one full meal, but eating between meals is forbidden. I once
thought that difficult. Yom Kippur makes the fasting in
Catholicism look like a banquet.

I was most fortunate to have a father-in-law like Sidney.
Over the years, and especially at the beginning of my Jewish
life, I turned to him for guidance and direction. I can't speak
for other converts, but having one's father-in-law as a mentor
was an opportunity I really appreciated. Going to shul with
him always made me feel more secure. He was there to guide
me through the services. He always had an answer and a
reason when I asked questions like, "Sidney, why aren't we
allowed to swim during the nine days leading up to *Tisha
B'av?*"

As I discovered, learning to be Jewish was not just a matter
of attending classes. At the age of thirty-two I was learning

a new way of life, attempting to eliminate bad habits and establish new ones. I had always enjoyed coffee with cream or milk after my meals. I knew one didn't drink milk with a meat meal, but I guess I hadn't realized that this statute applied to taking coffee with milk after eating meat, at least not for six hours. At first I found this to be a great inconvenience; I didn't like it. In time I began to realize its importance as a teaching device. Today, when I drink my coffee black or with a nondairy creamer, I am made aware of the scriptural injunction to be kind and devoid of all cruelty even to God's animals.

Yes, at times the practical living of Judaism can be burdensome, especially for someone who was not brought up in a Jewish home; it can be disruptive. But over the years one begins to feel comfortable in Judaism and begins to develop a "Jewish feeling" which at first did not exist. Even my attitude toward the land of Israel has changed from what it was in the beginning days of my Jewishness. Like many Americans I supported Israel, but I certainly did not feel obligated to fight to defend it or to send my son to war in its behalf. Over the last few years I can say that my attitude has turned completely around. I now have a deep feeling and love for Israel, one so strong that if called upon to defend it with my life I would do so; Israel is my home too.

It has taken many years to arrive at the state of Judaism I find in my life today, many years of hard work and persistency. But it has all been worth it, for today I can say, "I really am a Jew in mind, body, and soul."

From this perspective, and also from the perspective of my feelings twenty years ago when I emerged from the mikvah, my conversion has been a major source of happiness in my life. Not everyone shared in my joy, though. There were some at the seminary who would not speak to me when they became aware of my conversion. I especially remember one individual, today an ordained priest, who quite openly expressed his disgust.

I was visiting some of the seminarians at the house of studies on Monroe Street in Washington. One of them suggested that we go to a movie. We all piled into one of the cars. I was sitting in the back seat, and next to me was one of the students, who at this time was a deacon.

He turned to me and asked, "John, is it true that you converted to Judaism?" "Yes," I answered. At that, he abruptly got out of the car and went inside the house. One of the other seminarians followed and asked him what had happened. The deacon, I am told, said, "In good conscience I cannot sit next to John, nor will I ever speak to him again. He's a Judas, as far as I'm concerned."

Others would simply bid me the time of day and hurry past. I did not expect any of them to sanction what I had done, but on the other hand, I did not expect to be treated as though I had developed leprosy. I could see now that my relationships and friendships with my former "brothers in Christ" were abruptly ending. Till this day I have never heard from any of them.

I know men who left the priesthood to marry but were able to continue their friendships with those who remained in the seminary. This was not to be my experience. The realization that I would never be accepted by the men with whom I had lived for almost seventeen years was quite painful. Up to that time I had no friends in the secular world. I realized that all ties to my past life would now be severed. I accepted that, knowing that I would find acceptance in my new religion and would establish new friendships.

The task turned out to be greater than I had ever imagined. My courtship with Diane was not without much pain. Her parents, in spite of my conversion to Judaism, were not happy with our relationship. And I could understand that. What I could not understand was why they did not consider me a Jew like themselves. I assume that they looked upon my conversion as only a way to continue my relationship with Diane. There would be arguments, and invariably, in the heat of anger, a member of her family would refer to me as "the goy (Gentile)." I can't tell you how much that hurt. I began to feel like a "man without a country."

Later there were attempts to persuade me to change my last name. The argument most used was, "Well, if he honestly wants to be Jewish, then why does he keep his Gentile name?" I remember one incident in particular. One night Diane and I went to pick her mother up at a Hadassah meeting. Gertrude introduced Diane to some of the other women, and then she said, "And this is David Cohen, one of Diane's friends." Well, that infuriated me. In a loud voice I replied, "My name is not David Cohen, it's John Scalamonti!" And with that I stormed out and waited in the car.

But it was another incident, another remark, that caused me to wonder whether they really accepted me as a Jew. I don't think that anyone in Diane's family doubts the sincerity of my conversion any longer. There was a time, however, when they did, and some expected that I would either return to the church or attempt to convert Diane to Christianity. And, God forbid, that I might even baptize my children in secrecy. The many years since then have healed old wounds, and all of her relatives are more secure about my conversion now.

How was I and am I accepted by other Jews? Obviously I can only judge by the way people respond to me, and in all cases they seem to accept me. There was only one incident that might be considered negative. I was attending services on one of the festivals, I don't remember which, at Sidney's shul in Baltimore. Having only recently been converted, I had difficulty in following the services, and turned to a man sitting next to me, asking, "What page are we on?" He gave me the page number. I continued, "Thank you, I'm a recent convert and I'm not too familiar with the services as yet." Well, I expected him to respond positively, but instead he gave me a scowl and moved a few seats away from me.

For a while I began to wonder whether this was how I

would be treated by most born Jews. Fortunately, though, the small number of negative responses was more than outweighed by the many positive ones, especially among the rabbis and students I have met at the yeshiva in Lakewood, New Jersey. They, more than any others, have treated me with respect and have accepted me as a fellow-Jew.

Well, how did my family respond? In the next chapter I will deal with their initial reactions in greater detail. But here I would tell a bit about the sense of my family and their response to my conversion over the long term. I think I can honestly say that to this day they have never really accepted it and do not look upon me as a Jew.

I suppose it would be asking too much for them to make such an acknowledgment. In light of the attitudes of my friends and even of Diane's relatives, how could I expect more from my own family? To them I will always be John the priest, the good one who was led astray.

I don't doubt for a moment that when they heard of my conversion, they envisioned the following scene: This Jewish girl and some of her friends were visiting churches to find priests they could take away from their vocation and eventually convert to Judaism. They came upon the church where I was saying mass. Diane saw me and decided that she wanted to make me give up Christ and become a Jew. Imagine how great a mitzvah it would be for her to land a priest in the Jewish fold. What a great reward would she receive from the rabbis!

Maybe a little far-fetched, but not that far removed from what they believe happened. In their minds, I could never, on my own, have given up the priesthood to become a Jew. After all, I had never told them of my doubts concerning my priesthood and my faith. Maybe if I had been more honest with them, and prepared them for what happened, their imaginations wouldn't have run wild. I accept the blame and responsibility for being a coward. The fact is that as far as they are concerned, I converted in order to marry Diane. On a lighter note, I once reminded my mother about the times, years ago, when she would say to my younger brothers, "Find yourselves a rich Jewish girl and get married." "Yes," she said. "But I never meant it for you."

There have been several incidents that reflect their nonacceptance of my Jewishness. Whenever I return home for a visit, I always take Diane and the children, and we always bring our own kosher food. On one occasion, though, when an aunt died, I returned home alone for the funeral. After the funeral the family hosted a brunch at a local restaurant. When we got there, several of my relatives said, "Now you can eat whatever you want, Diane isn't here." I responded that I observed the dietary laws whether she was with me or not; I don't think I convinced them that I was serious about being a Jew, but at least there have been no more attempts to make me eat nonkosher food.

To be honest, I no longer try to make them understand that I became a Jew by choice. They have attended the Bat Mitzvahs of my two daughters and the bris of my son. By doing so they have demonstrated their respect for us, if nothing else.

We join in family celebrations on neutral grounds. By that I mean, we never visit them during the Christmas or Easter holidays, and renew our family ties during secular holidays, such as Memorial Day. In this way no one has to be uncomfortable and our visits remain strictly familial.

They will call to wish us a happy Hanukah or a happy Passover. We in turn call them at Christmas and Easter with our good wishes. This seems to work out very well. My children most certainly recognize my parents as their grandparents, and my parents love my children as they do their other grandchildren.

When I speak before Jewish groups, I am almost always asked why I do not take my children to my parents' home during the Christmas season. I answer, first, by reminding the audience that my marriage is not a mixed marriage. My family and I are Jewish, and as Jews we do not in any way celebrate the religious meaning of the Christmas season. Other Jews by choice, so I am told, participate in the Christian holiday with their Christian parents. I think, however, that while they are doing so for the sake of peace within the family, they may be sacrificing what is best for their children.

The road for a convert to Judaism is not an easy one. Years of living as a Jew must go by before the convert finds his or her place in the House of Israel. Questions concerning the convert's sincerity will be asked by both Christian and born Jew. And the convert must be ever so careful to avoid any innocent remark or action that may be construed as a sign that deep down he is still a Christian.

Why do born Jews so severely question the sincerity of the Jew by choice? Is it because they think so little about their own religion? One thing is certain: you won't find Christians acting that way when a Jew converts to Christianity. They are ecstatic over conversions to the faith, viewing them as a great blessing from God.

Very often the whole Christian community attends the baptism of a convert to witness it and make him feel welcome. The convert to Judaism, however, goes alone, almost in secrecy, to his or her immersion in the mikvah of conversion. Can't something be done to involve the Jewish community in such an event? Do converts have to be labeled "Jews by choice"? I have no doubt that the intentions of those who have proposed this designation are honest and sincere, but it seems to me that we already have enough labels in Judaism and don't need to add yet another. A Jew is a Jew in his heart and before his God. We are all children of Abraham. Why single anyone out by assigning him a label?

Through the twofold ritual of conversion I am a Jew. In the last analysis it matters not whether my family or other Jews accept this. What matters is what is in my heart and how I live my Jewish faith, and only our Heavenly Father knows that, and only He is the One Who counts.

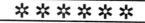

Dear Mom

People always ask, "How did you tell your parents about your conversion and what did they say?"

August, 1972

Dear Mom, Dad and family,

I hope that this letter finds you all in the very best of health. I am fine and in good health. There are several things that I have to tell you about.

First, I have decided not to return to the priesthood. This has not been an easy decision for me, but I have not been happy with my life there.

I have met a girl that I really love. We have been going out for some time now. I met her parents and they have been very good to me. We are not married or even engaged, but maybe it will end up there.

You should know that I have converted to Judaism. It is a beautiful religion and, I believe, the true one.

I didn't have the nerve to tell you these things in person or even over the phone. I hope you will understand. Thank you for all your support.

All my love, your son,
John

P.S. I'll understand if you never want to see me or speak to me again.

With this letter I told my mother and family about the changes that had occurred in my life. I didn't have the nerve or guts to tell her in person. I believed that when she received this letter I would never see or hear from my family again. But I had to do what I believed was right, regardless of the consequences.

This chapter is dedicated to my mother, to my mother-in-law, and to all mothers who have at one time or another received news from their children that caused them hurt which time alone will never totally heal.

I do not believe that any child sets out in life to deliberately hurt his mother and family. If anything, the opposite is true. We spend so much of our time during our childhood and even during adulthood trying to please our mothers. They are, after all, one of the greatest gifts that God has given to us. They are the ones responsible for our being here. They have nurtured us from birth and continue to nurture us with their love and support through life's experiences. It is, in most cases, the mother who is at the center of the family, supporting the weaker of her children and encouraging the stronger ones. Sadly, when she is gone from us, the family seems to lose the strong sense of unity it once possessed. The family isn't the same anymore, the children go their separate ways. Such is the power and influence of a mother's love over her family.

It was knowing that my mother was so proud and so filled with joy on the day of my ordination that enhanced my own joy even more. It was knowing that my leaving the priesthood would cause her great sorrow that held me back from making such a decision earlier. Before I took my leave of absence I once intimated to my father, as he was driving me to the airport to return to the seminary, that I was considering leaving the priesthood.

The first words out of his mouth were, "John, you know what this will do to your mother. It could break her heart." That's all I needed to hear.

He then asked me why I wanted to leave. I told him I wasn't happy and had problems in some areas of my faith. I knew he felt a sympathetic understanding of my predicament, but he reiterated the effect such a decision would have on my mother, so I dropped the topic. He would be uncomfortable about my leaving the priesthood but would be able to live with it. But could she?

Later, at some point, I told my brother Michael that I was thinking of leaving. He responded in much the same way as my father. "John, it's okay with me. Whatever you decide to do I'll support you. But you know if you left it will kill Ma." And so I never approached my mother with my decision to leave. This was before I ever met Diane and her family, and certainly before I converted. For that period of time I lived a lie. I remained in the priesthood, going through the motions of my priestly duties, until I finally took the steps to leave. After I had converted, I finally decided to tell my mother and family what I had done. But how to tell them?

And so I found myself caught, as they say, between a rock and a hard place. What could I do that would lessen the pain in my heart without causing even more pain in hers? There was no easy answer. It would be bad enough just to tell her I had left the priesthood. It would be even worse to tell her that I was in love with a girl; I knew she would blame her for my problems. But how would I tell her all this and then add, "Oh, one more thing, I've converted to the Jewish faith." I could not find the strength within me to go there in person and have to see the pain in her eyes. For that reason I decided to write the "Dear Mom" letter. It was an easy way out for me.

I mailed the letter and then waited, week after week, for my phone to ring. It never did. I believed that I had cut myself off from them forever. However, I had done what I believed was right. And it was this power of conviction that gave me the strength to do what I had to, just as it did when I decided to enter the seminary in spite of my mother's objections. I was beginning a new life, and although I would have wanted my mother and family to tell me that it was okay and they still loved me, I knew they probably would not. I could understand this. And so I was mentally prepared for this separation from them to occur. What I was not prepared for was a surprise visit from home.

Weeks had gone by since I mailed the letter and no response from home. One day there was a knock on my apartment door. I got up and looked through the peephole. There on the other side of the door, standing in the hall, were my three brothers, Michael, Andrew, and Charley. My God, I thought, they're going to make me go back home with them.

I let them in, asking, "How did you find me?" They told me that they had my return address from my letter and had taken a gamble that I would be in. Fortunately, I was off from work that day.

My brother Andrew served as the spokesman. He said that my mother had sent them down to see if I was still mentally and physically sound. I was happy to see them, at least I could talk to them about what I had done. Also, they would have a chance to meet Diane.

My brothers Mike and Charley were easy going. Charley especially let me know that he loved me. Andrew was a different story. He came in angry. He was very upset about what I had done and minced no words in telling me how our mother felt when she read my letter. As I had figured, leaving the priesthood was a mild thing, even having a girl was okay, but becoming a Jew . . . !

"How could you give up something you've believed in since you were a kid?" Andrew asked. He continued, "I just don't understand how you, a priest, could become a Jew."

No amount of logic or reason was going to satisfy him. As far as he was concerned, what I had done made no sense whatsoever, and he had to vent his anger and frustration about it. Andrew tried to talk me into coming home to live.

Maybe there I would return to my senses. I guess he felt that I was lost and confused. Why else, he must have told himself, would Johnnie, who was always such a good boy, have done such a thing?

At that point I decided it was time for them to meet Diane. I told them to wait in the apartment and I drove over to the college, which was but a block away. There I found Diane and told her about the surprise visit. She agreed to meet them.

I could see that they liked her the minute they saw her. Andrew, at first, showed resentment toward her, but she was able to hold her ground. Eventually he became her favorite brother-in-law, and till this day he respects and likes her. I spent time explaining to them the events that had changed my life.

Now that things had quieted down, I told them how happy I was being Jewish and how I had come to believe in Judaism. I know they didn't understand everything I was saying, but at least they saw that I wasn't insane. To the contrary, they saw how happy I was, and I think at that point they gave me their support.

Since they were planning to return home that day, I thought it would be a good idea for them to meet Mr. and Mrs. Max. Diane called her parents and asked them if it would be okay to stop in for a brief visit. This would give her parents an opportunity to at least meet and get to know some of my family.

Gertie not only agreed but insisted on preparing dinner for them. You guessed it, spaghetti and meatballs. And so we headed up Route 95 to Baltimore. Diane and I rode in my car, and my brothers followed.

When we arrived at Diane's home, Gertie was at the door to welcome them. She was terrific. She treated them with unbelievable kindness and respect. One incident during their visit that day I will always remember, and so will my 'ounger brother Charley. He was an excellent football player

who had won many awards, including five full-paid scholar-
ships. When Gertie found this out she went into the den. I
heard her speaking to someone on the phone. Soon she
came back into the dining room, a big smile on her face.

"Charley," she asked, "have you ever met a real professional football player?"

"No," he answered, "I've never had the chance to meet a
pro."

"Well, today is your lucky day. Bubba Smith lives across
the street, how would you like to meet him?"

I could see my brother's face light up. I think we were all
surprised and excited. Gertie had called Bubba while we
were eating and told him about Charley. She asked if he
would be kind enough to have Charley meet him. He agreed.
So after dinner we all went over to Bubba Smith's house. I
too, was excited about meeting him, but no one's excitement
could compare to Charley's. He still talks about the experience and how good it was of Mrs. Max to set up the visit for
him.

Weeks went by after my brothers left that evening. I knew
for sure that they would have nothing but good to say about
Diane and her parents, and I had high hopes that when they
returned home and told my mother about their visit with
her and her family, the gulf between us would be bridged.
Looking back, I know I should have made an attempt at
reconciliation, but fear of rejection and of hearing how much
I had hurt her caused me to do nothing. So as the weeks
went by without anything happening I decided that my
brothers' visit was the last I would see them.

Then, one morning, the phone rang.

"Hello," "Johnnie?" It was my mother.

"Well, since Mohammed wouldn't come to the mountain,
I guess the mountain has to go to Mohammed." That was
how she began her conversation with me. I remember saying
that I hadn't called because I thought she wouldn't want to
hear from me.

She began to cry. "Why would you think that?" she asked. "Don't you know that I'm still your mother and you are still my son? After all, you didn't kill anyone."

At that point I too broke into tears. I couldn't believe that she still loved and accepted me after what I had done and the way I had done it.

She continued, "Your brothers told me about Diane and her parents. They sound like wonderful people. Charley still can't get over that he met Bubba Smith."

And then came the words that began the much-needed healing and reconciliation. "Why don't you bring Diane home to meet us? I would really like to see her."

I couldn't believe what I was hearing. Was it possible that I still had a family? I said that we'd be glad to come for a visit. Again I told her how sorry I was for hurting her. I must have thanked her a million times for calling, and especially for inviting me back home with the girl I loved.

I was eager to tell Diane the news. She was happy to hear that my mother and family were still talking to me, and she was eager to visit them and see the place where I grew up as a young boy. Gertie and Sidney were also happy that I had spoken to my mother. "You have a wonderful mother," Gertie said. "I don't know if I would have been so forgiving."

I found the visit home enjoyable yet at the same time uncomfortable. Enjoyable because now the truth was out. Enjoyable because they seemed to accept Diane so well. Even my grandmother, to my surprise, seemed to have no problem with my leaving the priesthood. She also seemed sincerely happy for me and took a special liking to Diane. In Slovak she would call Diane, "My little Jewish girl." Uncomfortable, though, because my family had never seen me with a girl, much less one I looked at so lovingly. As a priest I always came home alone and had given them my undivided attention and love. Now I was sharing that love with another. So yes, there were moments when I felt uncomfortable and even awkward. But in time I would become more comfortable with my new way of life, and so would they.

Remarkably, no one asked about my conversion or why I had converted to Judaism. I suppose in their minds Diane was the reason. Diane, however, was deluged with questions about Judaism, and I must say she handled herself remarkably well. I was proud of her and the good impression she made.

On the surface it appeared that Diane and I could now pursue a normal relationship. Our parents knew we were seeing each other. The tremendous burden of having to tell my family of my decisions was lifted. They now knew that I was no longer a priest, had converted to Judaism, and was dating Diane. It appeared that a period of calm was setting in.

However, this was not to be the case. Both families were simply waiting for either Diane or myself to come to our senses. My family probably felt that in time I would get tired of working, realize I had made a mistake, and return to the church and the priesthood. Diane's family, I'm sure, were hoping Diane would realize that although I was a good person, I could not offer her a secure future. That even though we were now of the same religion, our cultural backgrounds were different. They encouraged her to continue dating Jewish boys who were either medical or dental students.

Esther, Diane's sister, was also very much against our relationship. She once wrote Diane a five-page letter listing all the reasons why Diane should not see me. I recently was shown the letter, and here is some of what she wrote: "How stable is this person? To become a priest and then decide it's a joke is an escape from something else, deeper than we know." I guess she was trying to indicate that I was having mental problems. She continues, "Is he a professional? How will you feel in your heart when you go to his family and your children see a Christmas tree?" Well, as I have already mentioned we never visit my parents' home during the Christmas and Easter seasons. I know that Esther had good intentions. She was concerned about her younger sister and wanted what was best for her. If anything, she deserves praise for taking the risk of confronting Diane.

In time both families realized that Diane and I were serious about each other. I was serious about my Judaism as well, trying to be observant but realizing that I had a long, long way to travel before I would achieve that goal. Our courtship had many ups and downs, usually because of family members. But Diane and I both believed we were right for each other. On Thanksgiving day I asked Sidney for her hand in marriage and presented her with an engagement ring (which I'd had her mother pick out for me), thus taking the first step that would eventually lead to the exchange of new vows.

✼ ✼ ✼ ✼ ✼ ✼

New Vows

Harai at mekudeshet lee, b'ta-ba-at zu, k'dat Mosheh v'Yisrael ("Be sanctified to me with this ring in accordance with the law of Moses and Israel").

With this declaration and her consent, Diane became my wife, according to the law of Moses and Israel. And so for me a new vow was taken, one not made to an institution or religious order, but to another person whom I love. With the support and consent of our families, Diane and I began, according to Jewish tradition, a new family.

The wedding was performed by Rabbi Samuel Rosenblatt in accordance with the prescribed rituals of Orthodox Judaism. It was a profoundly happy occasion for us, and was made even happier by the attendance not only of good friends but my entire family. There is no question about the goodness of our families. Would that the weddings of my children be as happy and joyful. Diane and I will always be grateful to our parents for making this occasion such a happy one for us.

So often, when I share my life's story with a Jewish audience, someone will come up to me in private and relate the sad experiences of a child or close relative who has married outside the Jewish faith. How painful for the parents who attend the ceremony, and how painful for the couple whose parents decide not to attend. Instead of a simcha (joy), there is sorrow and hurt. I hear their pain as they

154

relate the circumstances surrounding the wedding of their son or daughter. So great is the hurt that sometimes the parents never speak to their child again. Some have not even seen their first grandchild.

I hear these stories and realize how blessed Diane and I have been. I wish I could heal the wounds and take away the hurt of those who tell me these stories, but I can't. They have been deprived of witnessing the marriage of their son or daughter under the *hupah*.

Time alone will determine whether the hurt caused by one's children marrying outside the Jewish faith will be healed. But I do know and believe that we should never stop trying to bring them back to the House of Israel. As parents we must be there to welcome their return. We must show our opposition to their actions, but we should never withhold our love for them.

Back in 1982, when I was deputy mayor of Aberdeen, New Jersey, a Jewish mother asked me to perform a civil marriage ceremony for her daughter, who was marrying a Gentile. I knew that the mother was hurt and upset. Being more directed by my heart, I agreed to perform the ceremony.

The mother asked me to interject some elements of Jewish prayer into the ceremony, so that she could feel that the marriage had a semi-religious sanction of some kind, and for her sake, I agreed to do it. I have seen the mother many times since that day. Recently she told me that her daughter and son-in-law had become the proud parents of a baby girl; moreover, they had brought the child to temple for naming and intended to bring her up in the Jewish faith.

Certainly all this falls short of what is required by Jewish law as prescribed by Moses and tradition. I do not regret what I did at that time, but now, having become more observant and more educated in the teachings of the Torah and the Talmud, I would no longer participate in the marriage of a Jew and a Gentile.

At the beginning of our marriage Diane and I were busy

trying to build a kosher and Jewish home. She was occupied with setting up her kitchen, carefully arranging the drawers for the dairy and meat utensils and making room in the cabinets for the meat and dairy dishes. I was proud and happy to be able to preside over our Shabbos dinner. There seemed to be an added dimension in being a Jewish husband.

Yes, it is true that being a husband, whether Jew or Gentile, brings with it the basic obligations of providing for a wife and family. And both Jew and Gentile are bound by the marriage vows, which require faithfulness. But the Jewish husband is all this and more. He is the religious leader of the home. He is the religious authority to whom his wife and children look for direction, religious standards, and encouragement in the living of their faith. He is, or should be, the source of religious inspiration and observance.

The Jewish husband is the breadwinner who provides food not only for the family's physical nourishment, but for its spiritual sustenance. It is his duty, as husband and father, to ensure that those entrusted to his care follow the laws and commandments, so that Israel and the world will become holy. "You shall be holy, for I, the Lord your God, am holy" (Leviticus 19:2). And again "You shall be to Me a kingdom of priests and a holy nation" (Exodus 19:6). I see the Jewish husband and father as the "priest" of his household, leading his small flock to a life of holiness.

For Diane and myself, married life was an adjustment, as it is for all who enter this sacred and human union. Marriage is a union that requires unselfish love and mutual commitment; a union that should reflect the eternal covenant made centuries ago between God and His people. In Judaism, as I see it, marriage has its own meaning and significance quite apart from the aspect of having children. Propagating the species is a fundamental biblical precept, but side by side with this, love and companionship are in themselves valid reasons for two human beings to come together as husband

and wife. In Catholicism, by contrast, marriage exists first and foremost for the procreation of children. Thus Judaism treats sexual relations between husband and wife positively and in a favorable light, whereas Catholicism merely condones them as a necessary evil.

At this time I was employed by Gino's Fast Food. I had been hired to become a regional human-resources manager, but first had to work in their restaurants as a manager. This was very difficult for us. Many times I was required to work on Friday nights, Diane, in consequence, had to spend Shabbos night alone. This was very painful but necessary if I was to make a living and eventually earn promotion to a position which would allow me nights and weekends off.

Since Diane was working as a teacher in a day-care school, we sometimes hardly saw each other. She would be off on weekends, when I was working. Her hours were nine to four on weekdays, and I often had to leave for work before she came home and then did not get back till after midnight.

Our observance of Judaism in those days was limited to keeping kosher both at home and outside. Our observance of Shabbos was, unfortunately, restricted by my job. Whenever I could get a weekend off, however, we would drive out to Diane's parents' home on Friday afternoon and spend Shabbos with them, attending services at their shul, which was but a few blocks away. I always looked forward to these visits because they made it possible for me to spend time discussing Torah and Judaism with my father-in-law. His inspiration made me all the more anxious to have my own family, and to have a job that would allow me to observe Shabbos properly. Little did I know that Diane and I would soon be welcoming the first member of our family and thus that part of my wish would be fulfilled.

✿ ✿ ✿ ✿ ✿ ✿

They Call Me Abba

How often, as a priest, did I long to have my own children. When I visited my brothers and played with their kids, the full meaning of the sacrifice of celibacy came home to me. How beautiful a gift from God was a newborn infant.

When I returned home to perform the baptismal ceremony for my brother Michael's firstborn son, the first thing I did, after stopping briefly at my parents' house, was to go over to Michael's place to see the new arrival. Lifting him from his crib, I turned to my brother, saying, "Mike, you have everything right here. What I wouldn't give to have a baby boy like this."

How well do I remember that ceremony, not only because it was my nephew whom I was baptizing, but because it was the first baptism I performed as a priest. I was more nervous than the parents and god-parents. As I anointed his tiny forehead with holy oil, I thought about how beautiful he was and how I wished he were mine. My heart welled with love for him when I poured the baptismal water on his head and he began crying.

Over the years, I baptized many other babies, and on each occasion I could not help but reflect on the sad thought that I would never have a child of my own. Yes, I was called "father," and spiritual father I was to all children and to all members of the Catholic church, young and old. I suppose I derived some degree of solace from my priestly designation as "father," but certainly not near enough to placate the desire of natural fatherhood. I resigned myself to the reality of my life; I would be called "father" but would have no one of my own flesh and blood to call son or daughter.

On the day of my ordination, I was quite certain that nothing else in life could possibly equal or surpass the joy and happiness I was experiencing. But that is just what happened to me when I held my firstborn in my arms. My joy on that day was infinitely greater and more powerful than what I had felt on being ordained. I had become the father of a baby girl, a new life—something I had once never imagined to be possible. Holding my own child in my arms, I could now say with a new and dearer meaning the words I had once uttered at mass, "This is my flesh, this is my blood."

Little Dina Leah's naming took place at my father-in-law's shul. Three more times God blessed Diane and myself with children. We had two more daughters, Chana Rivka and Shana Hyah Masha, and then came a son, who at his bris was named Daniel Mordecai. And so my life had now taken on an added dimension. I who once was "father" to strangers had become "abba" to my own children.

People often ask me how my children feel about the fact that I was once a priest. Fortunately, Diane and I have never had any difficulty in explaining my former life. Nor have our children had any problems in accepting or understanding who and what I was. At the same time they are fully aware that my family is Catholic, celebrating different holidays, eating different foods, praying and worshiping in a different way.

Before Diane and I married, we were often warned that our children would be confused as to what religion to practice and believe; they might be influenced by their Catholic relatives, we were told. My response then and now is that if any confusion entered their minds, it would not be because of my family's practices, beliefs, or influence, but because of the influence of non-observant Jews.

My family has never attempted to influence my children or draw them away from Judaism. My mother has never tried to baptize them in the kitchen sink, as someone once said would happen. My relatives respect my children's faith and admire the fact that they are observant, that they know what kosher is and practice it. They sense and respect their deep Jewish faith.

No, the difficulties we sometimes experience in trying to educate them to be observant Jews come not from Gentiles but from other Jewish children who are nonobservant. Many times have my children been invited to the birthday party of a Jewish friend only to have to turn down the invitation because the party was being held at a McDonald's or some other unkosher restaurant. What do you answer when your children ask, "If Mark is Jewish, how come he can eat a Big Mac or a cheeseburger?" Or, "How come Melissa has a Christmas tree?" When my children were small, I made a point of not visiting my family during the Christmas and Easter holidays, so as to ensure that they were not exposed to anything that might confuse them about who they are and what religion they are to practice. Today, even though they are older, we still do not celebrate Christian holidays with my family.

I think we Jewish parents make a mistake when we try to compensate our children for not having Christmas by making Hanukah its Jewish equivalent. Remember, for Christians, Christmas is one of the major holidays of the year, the other being Easter. For us Jews, Hanukah is only one of several minor holidays. If you want your children to be able to deal with Christmas, teach them to appreciate and enjoy the many Jewish festivals and holidays all through the year. Keeping them home from school to attend shul and celebrate our holidays helps them to define their Jewishness and to express their Jewish identity with dignity.

As a Jewish parent, and maybe, too, because I am a convert, I think it very important for our children to participate in every Jewish festival and holiday. Observing our holidays will strengthen their self-identity as Jews in a society that is overwhelmingly non-Jewish. This was the experience of our ancestors over four thousand years ago, and it is our experience today.

Friday nights are always special to us as a family. During the day and when the children come home from school, we all make a special effort to prepare our home for the celebration of Shabbos. And then we begin our Shabbos with the lighting of candles. When I watch my wife, now accompanied by two of our daughters, performing this ceremony, and think back to my first experience of it twenty years ago in her parents' house, I am always very moved. And we have yet another daughter who soon will be sharing in this beautiful event.

The light from so many burning candles fills our home with a certain warmth and splendor. We strive to make this night special. We believe it important that our children know and feel that welcoming Shabbos and sharing in the Shabbos meal is one of the most important events of the week. It is from this sacred event that we as a family are renewed in our Judaism and find the strength and encouragement to practice our faith. For me it becomes the highest expression of what being a Jewish father and husband is all about. Through the observance in our home we as parents fulfill, at least partially, the commandment, "Make it known to your children and to your children's children" (Deuteronomy 4:9).

I have written about the importance Judaism gives to home and family. This side of Judaism has always been very attractive to me, and the role of husband and father, as I have explained, has been very meaningful, but I also want to say something about my discovery of Judaism as a community religion.

Unlike Christianity or Islam, Judaism was first experienced by a community, a people, rather than by individuals. Judaism is the only religion that can trace its origin to the spiritual-historical event that occurred at Mount Sinai. There, thousands of our ancestors witnessed the promulgation of the Ten Commandments, ratifying, by their acceptance of the Law, the covenant between God and His people. The very existence of Judaism rests upon the historical event in which the Law was given and accepted by this new nation, this new people, this "faith-nation."

Because of its unique origin, Judaism is much more a community religion than a family one, although without the Jewish home the community itself would diminish. At the same time, it is from the community that we as a people draw strength and receive direction in the living out of our Jewish faith. My family receives strength from the daily home observances of our faith, but after worshiping with our local community we come home with renewed love and a desire to all the more observe our Judaism in our family. The sense of unity experienced in the shul encourages and inspires us to an even greater love and appreciation for our faith and Jewish heritage.

The focal point for the Jewish community is the synagogue, or shul. The first time I entered a shul happened to be during the Passover holidays. My father-in-law took me with him to his shul, Tifereth Israel, on Greenspring Avenue in Baltimore. As we entered, my attention was immediately focused on the *ner tamid*, or eternal lamp, which reminds us, as I learned later on, of God's presence in His sacred word, the Torah. It attracted me because it was so familiar. All Catholic churches have an eternal lamp as a reminder of the presence of God in the consecrated bread used for the eucharist. I said to Sydney, "They have the same lamp in Catholic churches." And he replied with a smile, "I guess they got it from us."

I was also struck by the separation of men and women.

Not because I found it odd but because in my parish church back home the practice of men and women sitting on separate sides was the custom. I always sat with my father and brothers on the "men's side," as we called it. Again, a familiar tradition.

While living in Greenbelt, Maryland, in the early years of our marriage, Diane and I did not formally become members of a congregation. We generally attended services at a shul near our apartment or at her father's shul when in Baltimore. Most people were not aware of my background, but some members of Sidney's shul, including the rabbi, were. They always treated me with great kindness and respect. Never once was I made to feel like an outsider.

It wasn't until 1977 that Diane and I finally became members of our own shul. At that time my company offered me a position as regional personnel manager for northern New Jersey. We didn't like the idea of leaving Maryland and Diane's parents, but the benefits of the new position outweighed the negatives. It would allow us the opportunity to be together for Shabbos every Friday night and to attend shul on Saturday.

Our new home was in Aberdeen, formerly called Matawan. There we were welcomed into Congregation Bet Tefilah by Rabbi Sokoloff. I found him to be a true Jew—honest, kind, and truly exhibiting the teachings of Torah. He went out of his way to give me special attention and see to it that I was involved in the shul's activities. Thanks to him I began attending the weekday minyan for the daily *shaharit* service. He appointed me to the school committee, and I am proud to say that because of our efforts to establish a day school, Bayshore Hebrew Academy exists today. All of my children have received their Jewish educations at Bayshore Hebrew. Because of Rabbi Sokoloff, I also began studying Hebrew and Torah in more depth by attending the yeshiva in Lakewood, New Jersey.

There is no doubt that Rabbi Sokoloff's influence and

direction made me a more observant Jew. He took the time
to show me the way and often encouraged me while on that
way. He has since left our shul, but I will always remember
him for the kindness and love he gave me and my family. In
his place a new rabbi has come, Rabbi Kruptka, a man cut
from the same cloth. He too encourages and instructs me in
the ways of Judaism. He too has shown me much kindness
and respect, and urges me to participate fully in the life of
the shul. How fortunate for me to have met such wonderful
teachers who not only with words but by actions showed me
what being Jewish means.

So it is that my wife and I provide for our children the
fullness of a Jewish life. A home in which their daily life is
lived as a Jew, and a shul where they receive the religious
instruction and education necessary for their faith to grow,
and find a community of love from which their faith receives
its nourishment.

Often I am asked whether I will allow my children to date
Gentiles? And as often as I am asked this question, my
response is always a firm no. The questioner probably feels
that I would be lenient about interdating because I was once
a Gentile and Diane went out with me. But assuming that
my past experience would be the determining factor entirely
misses the point. The fact that I was a Gentile at one time in
no way diminishes what I believe to be best for my children
and their Jewish faith. When I converted, I declared, as Ruth
did, "Your people are my people, and your God is my God"
(Ruth 1:16).

Often, too, I tell those who ask this question that the
often-voiced argument, "I'm only going to go out with him/
her one time. We're not going to get married," does not ring
true. Look at what happened to Diane, I say. I was the first
and only Gentile she dated. I know that when she agreed to
go out with me she never intended to fall in love or to marry,
but it happened. Fortunately, and thanks to God, it worked
out well for her, but such is not often the case.

Dating must be recognized as a form of courting. Even as a priest I knew that allowing children of different faiths to date opens the door for many problems to develop. Marriages between Catholics and Protestants—the kind of inter-marriages I dealt with then—posed problems enough, and both parties were Christians! Marriages between Jews and Christians are even more difficult, especially when there is no conversion and the couple foolishly tries to bring their children up in both religions, to make a choice later on. Such children, in truth, are being brought up in no religion.

There are no guarantees that my children or yours will do what we want them to do. But this in no way diminishes our solemn duty as parents to instill in them a love and warmth for the Jewish faith. This can only be done by creating an atmosphere of love and deep appreciation for Judaism and things that are Jewish. Making Shabbos and observing kashrut, making Friday nights special and warm, creating a consciousness of Jewish rituals and obligations, a knowledge of Jewish history—all this helps to lessen the chances that our children will marry outside the Jewish faith.

Certainly it is not easy to be a father in today's world, but to be blessed with good children is very rewarding. Being a Jewish father is even more difficult because of the responsibility of seeing to it that the faith of Abraham is preserved and continues intact into the next generation. When this happens, then the father's reward is doubled. Thus, when my children call me "abba" (father), my title represents for me not only the biological fact of fatherhood, but, in a very real way, the spiritual fatherhood of God.

Filling The Vessel

It has been nearly twenty-four years since my ordination to the priesthood and twenty years since my acceptance into the House of Abraham. My life appears to me at times to resemble that of a mountain climber, which happens to be the meaning of my last name. *Scalare* means "to climb," and *monte* means "mountain;" thus Scalamonti, "to climb the mountain."

As a boy I stood at the bottom of a mountain and looking up to the top saw a bright light. I decided to climb the mountain to get closer to the light and see what it was. After years of hard work and discipline my lonely journey to the top seemingly ended. But after a few more years, the light, which I had believed to be true and eternal, began to grow dim, and upon further and closer inspection I realized that it was simply a manmade reflection of the One, True Light. Soon it diminished, and in the darkness that surrounded me I stumbled and fell down the other side of the mountain. I found myself at the bottom in a state of utter despair, a blind man with no sense of direction. Thanks to God and His wondrous ways, a family of Abraham took me in. They gave me love and acceptance, and because of their acts of kindness I was once again able to see the brilliance of the light, first from the Shabbos candles and now on the mountain's top. And so I have begun another journey up the mountain. I have far, so far, to go before I reach the summit. But I know

now that I am reaching the True Light. And on this journey I am not alone. For now my family is with me, and together, we hope, we will reach the top and stand in the splendor of the light.

For me, being a Jew is a constant state of becoming more Jewish. Some believe that simply being born a Jew is enough. Others believe that if you strictly observe the 613 mitzvot you have arrived at the top of the mountain. But these views are too static. Becoming a Jew denotes activity, growth, a process that requires work, study, discipline, and dedication. When I stepped out of the mikvah, I was like a newborn child, not yet a man but having the right and opportunity to become one.

The rite of conversion did no more than allow me to journey on the same path with God's Chosen. It was as though it had given me a vessel which now, by living the life prescribed by Torah, I must fill. And that is where I am today. Journeying in the world as one of God's Chosen, striving to become holy, attempting to fill the vessel in order to become a total Jew. The Torah guides and instructs me, it tells me which direction to take, and it even warns me of the consequences should I go a different way.

In the life of a Jew there are many opportunities to become more holy or to become less a Jew, depending on how we choose. And it is well for us to follow the admonition of Deuteronomy 30:19, "I have put before you life and death, blessing and curse. Choose life, if you and your offspring would live."

Some converts are attracted to Judaism because of its teachings regarding the sacredness of life, the value and dignity of the human person, the right of men and women to live in freedom. I, too, love the teachings of the Torah which instruct us to be kind, understanding, compassionate, and charitable. Some are attracted by the prescribed ritual observances and discipline, and in fulfilling them find a sense of self-righteousness. Sadly, some Jews and converts accept only the ethical teachings of Judaism and totally disregard the prescribed observances and halakhic principles. Others only keep the letter of the law, but refrain from the commandment to "love your neighbor as yourself."

To be truly Jewish, I have learned, one must accept and live both the ethical teachings of the Torah and the prescribed rituals and commandments. It is not enough for the Jew to love one's fellow man, for even the humanist does this. Nor is it enough to simply follow laws and rituals, for even pagans can do that.

To me Judaism is like wine in a wineskin: neither has meaning without the other. The wine is sweet and delicious to our senses, easy to swallow. It can be compared to the Torah's teachings on love, compassion, kindness, and forgiveness. The wineskin is hard and rough to the touch, and can be compared to the ritual observances and laws that the same Torah commands us to observe. To become holy, the Jew must carry both the wine and the wineskin on his journey. At times the wineskin's strap around our necks will be an irritant. It will call the attention of others, and some will look at us with amused curiosity, others with disdain, and some even with hatred. But such is the lot of the man and woman who are called to become holy, who are called to be Jews.

Accepting and living the ethical teachings of Judaism was easy for me, partly because of my nature and my early childhood. Accepting and bearing the wineskin was more difficult. My first painful experience with the total teachings of the Torah took place in regard to kashrut. Having lived in the Boston area for nine years, I had developed a great love for seafood, especially shrimp and lobster. Denying myself this forbidden food was and is a sacrifice. But I realized early that keeping kosher, no matter how much of a sacrifice it involved, would be the foundation for my observance of other religious rituals and commandments. It is a daily reminder to me of who and what I am. The observance of kashrut is the foundation of our Jewish home. Our children have accepted it from their earliest years, and I am happy to say that in spite of the many distractions from their peers, they have always observed it faithfully.

Kashrut has become, for our family, the indispensable element that makes our life distinctively Jewish. Keeping kosher tells our friends and neighbors that we are Jews and proud to be Jews. We see kosher food as God's food, and our table as His altar upon which this food is eaten. In participating in an act so commonplace as eating food, we are sanctifying the meal and are using kashrut as a means to attain holiness.

There is also a lot to be said for the way that keeping kosher and observing the other commandments helps to build character and strengthen discipline in our lives and our children's. There is an important human value in the observance of rituals and laws, the value of self-discipline. It helps us to resist other drives and urges which are not always good for us and can even lead us away from the Torah.

Shortly after my conversion I was surprised to discover that not all Jews observed the commandment of kashrut. I was truly surprised and couldn't understand why a Jew would not keep kosher. Some justify their indifference by claiming that keeping kosher is too hard or interferes with their social relationships. Others object that it is too expensive to keep a kosher home but think nothing of buying expensive clothes, cars, and homes. I feel sorry for those who feel this way. They have abandoned something that is essential to being fully Jewish, a religious observance that all Jews, regardless of denomination, should practice. For it is in observing the dietary laws that our Jewish identity becomes evident, not only to Gentiles but, more importantly, to ourselves.

Being Jewish means to constantly grow in one's Judaism, and as we all know, growth can be painful. Friday nights and Saturdays when I had to work in the restaurant were very painful for me. I could see how difficult, if not impossible, it must have been for the immigrant Jew coming to this land and finding himself working on Shabbos in order to support his family. How often the religious practices of his faith had to take second place. How difficult a dilemma; in so many cases it led inexorably to the deterioration of their own Jewish practices and, even more, those of their children.

It has been a good fourteen years since I had to work on Friday nights and Saturdays. Thanks to my promotion I was able to revive my religious practices. In 1983 I went a step further by giving up a relatively good job with a large corporation in order to establish my own business. In this way I was free to observe all the festivals and holidays without having to worry about losing my job. Now, on Fridays, I would be home in plenty of time to prepare for Shabbos or be able to help out at our shul when my services were required.

I know that I and my family have a long way to go before we reach the mountain's top. At times the climb can be discouraging, but looking back over the years of progress I had spent on the journey encourages me to continue. It is the constant reaffirmation of Judaism through the daily and weekly observances that will ultimately help me and my family to complete our climb. And even when we reach the summit, I know, we will have to study and labor even more intensely in order to remain there.

The Journey Continues

If someone had approached me back in 1967 and said, "John, someday you'll be a married man with a wife and four children." I would have told him that he didn't know what he was saying. And if someone, and I can't imagine who it could have been, had come up to me and said, "Listen, not only will you be married with a family but you'll be Jewish," I would reply in no uncertain terms that he was crazy. Because as you know by now, in 1967 I was a happy, committed, celibate, Roman Catholic priest. I never in my wildest imagination would have dreamed that someday I would be a Jew. Nor would I ever have imagined that I would take upon myself the task of extolling the teachings of Judaism to born Jews, trying to convince them to rededicate themselves to their religious heritage. Nor did I ever anticipate that I would someday write a book for Jews, again hoping that its contents would awaken their interest in their faith, making them more willing to answer the call to become "a holy nation," a holy people."

Over the past few years I have spoken before many Jewish groups, sharing with them my life's experience and my conversion to Judaism. I always do so in the hope that my story and message will persuade at least one member of the audience to go home more committed to Judaism, more renewed in faith. My intentions are honorable, and I find no need to denigrate my former religion in order to make

171

Judaism attractive, its beauty is not relative. My purpose is not to undermine the faith of those who believe in Christianity. I want only to share my religious experience with those who want to listen.

I believe that God, in His plan, has given me a new life and a new religion. In Judaism I have discovered the most perfect reflection of the One, True God. I have been allowed entrance into the Chosen People and have accepted the covenant made with Abraham. In Judaism I have found a religion which unites my human life with holiness. My belief in Judaism has motivated me to do whatever I can to promote the Jewish faith, not only to those who have already received it but even to those who demonstrate a desire to know more about it. There are many non-Jews who, through no fault of their own, do not know the truth of Judaism. There are Jews, too, who do not know the essence of their faith. What little I know of Judaism, what little I have experienced in Judaism, is enough for me to regret that I was not born a Jew, and enough for me to attempt to persuade those born in the faith to appreciate their religious heritage and live it to the fullest.

In some circles, due to the prejudice born of ignorance, Judaism is regarded as incomplete, unfulfilled, as a religion of the past and even as godless. To those who hold this view I say, Open your hearts and minds to the message God has given to all peoples through His Chosen Ones; see for yourselves what you have rejected. Often, in rejecting the messenger, the message too is rejected, and this must not happen.

Among Jews, in our so secular age, there is an ambivalent attitude toward the convert. People who feel secure in their Jewish identity without being religious, tend to be suspicious of one whose motives for joining the Jewish people are spiritual. They feel that he is not telling them the whole story—that religion alone would not make him take so drastic a step. Their doubts reflect the void in their own souls and show how much work there is to be done.

Judaism teaches that we are all God's children, Jew and Gentile. To paraphrase a teaching in the Talmud, all good men and women will share in the life of the world-to-come (Tosefta, Sanhedrin 13:2). But in the meantime we must live together in the only world we know.

At times many of us become lost during our journey on earth; like our ancestors, we become wanderers in the desert. And yet, as He did for them, God has provided us with "a cloud by day and a pillar of fire by night" (Exodus 13:21). His Scriptures are that cloud and that pillar of fire. The Bible is His plan for us, and the Talmud is our guidepost, pointing the way in which to live His plan.

Some of us have rejected the plan; others have rejected the guidepost and become lost, not knowing who they are or where they are going. It is time for those who cherish our faith to boldly reach out to those who are lost and to those who have rejected the faith. It is time for all of us to begin to live our lives according to God's plan and will, and in so doing we will become "a light unto the nations" (Isaiah 42:6, 49:6). To become holy and to sanctify this world is the mission which we have been given. To look upon the Garden of Eden not as part of man's past but rather as his future.

I have shared my story with you; until now it has been shared with only a few, but those few have convinced me that it should be made accessible to all Jews everywhere. If my words can but renew the spiritual life of one Jewish person, it would be as though they had spiritually renewed a Jewish world.

✥ ✥ ✥ ✥ ✥ ✥

Living Jewishly with John

I know Jewish couples who differ on how and what their children are to believe and practice in following the precepts of the Jewish faith. One parent observes the Sabbath, the other will have no part of it. One would like to keep a kosher home, but her husband discourages her from doing so. Often they will say, "I wish my husband was as Jewish as John." So all the old fears about John's conversion and belief in Judaism have been laid to rest. Now everyone marvels and tells me how lucky I am to have a husband who really tries to live his Jewish faith and sets such a good example to our children.

My sister and I were raised in a very Jewish home. We kept kosher and observed the holidays; beyond that we were less observant in many areas but we knew we were not to associate with Gentile boys and certainly never to date one. I held hard and fast to this unwritten rule. The boys I dated were only of the Jewish faith, although I will admit that some of them and their families were nonobservant. I used to worry about the possibility that if I married one of them it might be confusing for our children, for one parent would be observant and the other not. A husband of this type probably would have gone along with me in keeping a kosher home but would have done whatever he wanted outside the house. Regardless of this possibility, it was more acceptable and correct to marry a non-practicing Jew than to a Gentile.

At the time I met John, I was attending my last year of college at the University of Maryland. In order to help my parents defray the cost of school, I took a part-time job as a waitress at the Emerson Steak House in Silver Springs. As you already know, it was there that I met John. I would like to explain why it was that I accepted his invitation to dinner, why I violated the unwritten rule of my home and upbringing.

When John first came to work at the restaurant he became the topic of everyone's conversation. He was known as the ex-priest. Back then, leaving the priesthood was a rather rare occurrence, and it was even more rare to meet a former priest, let alone to have one as manager and boss. We all liked John because he was very fair and kind to all the employees. I never once entertained any thought, nor even a suggestion of one, that his relationship with me would be anything but work-related. His invitation to dinner caught me by surprise. I accepted without thinking, knowing that nothing would ever come of it; besides, I was curious about his past and thought it would be an interesting evening. I never dreamed that this one date with a non-Jew would be the beginning of a difficult relationship that would lead to marriage. Nor did I ever envision that because of our marriage John would one day become more Jewish than I and my family. I often wonder if God may have planned this to happen even though the rules would have never allowed it.

Our relationship was not an easy one. I felt very guilty dating John, and after his conversion the relationship was no less painful. I would ask my mother whether God would punish me for marrying him. She was always quick to respond that God doesn't work that way. Some of my former Jewish boyfriends would make remarks like, "Are you really going to marry that spaghetti bender?" Some of my relatives would point a finger of condemnation at me, "You're the first one in our family to marry a *goy*." Others would jokingly say, "Your children will be half-breeds." Thank God, they were all wrong.

At the very beginning of our marriage I felt quite needed in the area of religious instruction regarding the rituals and practices in our home. John was always eager and more than willing to learn and to accept correction when necessary. It seemed, however, that my explanations for certain practices were not enough for him. It wasn't enough for him to simply perform rituals and observances. He constantly wanted to know why, as if he wanted to go beyond the surface and into the essence of his new religion. It was then that he began on his own to study Judaism in some depth. I was happy to have him simply go along with the beliefs and practices I had learned from my mother and her family. What more did he need?

This year will be our nineteenth wedding anniversary. They have been nineteen years in which Judaism has grown in me because of John's influence. I was always aware of *how* one should be a Jew, but in living with him I have learned *why* I am and should be a Jew. I never believed it would be so, I never envisioned that a time would come in my life when his knowledge and practice of Judaism would surpass mine, who would have thought that I would learn about the essence of my religion from him?

It was especially when we moved to New Jersey and joined Congregation Bet Tefillah that John began to surpass me in observance and knowledge of Judaism. He became very involved with Rabbi Sokoloff and the shul. Soon he was attending Torah classes with students from the yeshiva. Whenever he was able he would join the minyan at shul for either *shahait* or *maariv*. He would always come home with some new discovery or new aspect of looking at Judaism. Often he would tell me how similar the morning and evening services at shul were to the morning and evening prayers in the seminary. At times, he would come home in a state of excitement because he had been given the honor of opening the ark or carrying the Torah.

I was never what you might call a real shul-goer. My appreciation for John's love of Judaism was seen more in my home and how he always attempted to make sure that our children participated in our rituals and observances. He took great care to make sure that they understood what the Seder meant to us as Jews and presided over the rituals ensuring their complete observance. It was at such times that I could see the former habits of the priest come out. He truly acts as a teacher of Judaism in our home.

Unlike the husbands of many of my Jewish friends, John has always seen to it that he is off from work on the holidays. He makes sure that all of us attend services on those occasions. We may not see eye to eye on other subjects, but the one area which has never caused division or argument has been our religious observance as a family. I guess I've been very lucky.

Even after John's conversion there were those close to me who questioned his sincerity and wondered aloud how long it would be before he went back to Catholicism. No matter what they said, I always believed that his conversion was genuine and he would never return to his former religion. Maybe I felt that way because fairly early in our relationship I had given his apartment a thorough lookover. We were on our way to my mother's for Passover and stopped there for him to pick up an extra suit. While he was getting his things together, I carefully looked around to see if there were any crosses or pictures to indicate that he still had some feeling for his former religion, but there was nothing. Because of that I really believed him when he said he had completely broken with Catholicism.

But I know now that it is not enough for John simply to be a good Jewish husband and father. I know how strongly he believes that Judaism is the most perfect of all religions. For this reason he feels strongly the need to meet with Jewish groups and relate to them his experience of Judaism. He shares his life's experience with them and wants them to appreciate more fully the Jewish faith which they were born into. I have seen how his audiences listen attentively to his words and message. Afterwards, people always come up and tell me what a wonderful speaker and person John is and how good he made them feel about being Jewish. At these times I feel so proud of him and see again how living Jewishly with John has been more fulfilling and rewarding than I ever could have expected. And I feel good that our children, because of him, have a genuine love and understanding of their Jewish faith, and God willing, will someday instill such an appreciation of Judaism in the lives of their children and their children's children.

Glossary

ABBA (Aramaic "father"): A term sometimes used as an honorary title for teachers of the Mishnaic and Talmudic periods. It was also used as a term to address God.

ALMAH (Heb. "young woman"): The word appears in the biblical verse "Behold a young woman shall conceive and bear a son" (Isaiah 7:14). The word has been mistranslated as "virgin" in many translations of the Bible.

BAT MITZVAH (Heb. "daughter of the commandment"): It refers to a girl who has attained her religious majority, usually at twelve years and one day, although the occasion is frequently marked at age thirteen in order to be parallel to the ceremony marking a boy's religious majority.

BETH DIN (Heb. "house of judgment"): It refers to a Jewish court of law. In Mishnaic and Talmudic times, the lowest court consisted of three judges, the next level court consisted of twenty-three judges, and the highest court (the Great Sanhedrin) consisted of seventy or seventy-one judges. In medieval and modern times, the courts sometimes varied from these sizes.

BRIS or BRIT (Heb. "covenant"): Usually refers to the agreement between God and Abraham or God and the Jewish people. It also is used as a shortened form for Brit Milah, the covenant marked by circumcision.

DAVENING: A word of Yiddish origin used to refer to the act of praying.

GOY (Heb. "people"): A term used in the Bible to refer to any nation. In later usage it came to refer solely to non-Jewish people.

HADASSAH: The Women's Zionist Organization of America is a nonprofit organization that raises money to support medical care and education programs in Israel and Jewish and Zionist education programs for adults and youth in the United States.

HAGGADAH (Heb. "telling"): The set text of the prayers and readings used during the Passover seder.

HALAKHAH, HALAKHIC (Heb. "law," "legal"): The body of Jewish civil, criminal, and religious law.

HALLAH: A term referring to the portion of dough that is separated as a gift for the priest in accordance with biblical law. It has come to refer also to the traditional Sabbath loaves, since the preparation of the loaves provides an opportunity to fulfill this requirement.

HAMETZ (Heb. "leaven"): A term referring to agents of fermentation and, by extension, products containing such agents. Leavening agents and leavened products are subject to rules prohibiting their use and possession during Passover.

HANUKKAH: An eight-day festival that celebrates the cleansing and rededication of the Temple in Jerusalem by Judas Maccabee on 25 Kislev 165 B.C.E.

HUPAH: The canopy under which the bride and groom stand during the marriage ceremony. The term is also sometimes used to refer to the ceremony itself.

179

KIDDUSH (Heb. "sanctification): The prayer recited over a cup of wine on the eve of a Sabbath or festival proclaiming the sanctity of the day.

KOSHER, KASHRUT (Heb. "fit," "fitness"): Food that is permitted under the system of Jewish dietary laws.

MAARIV: The evening service, which is recited daily after nightfall.

MATZAH: Unleavened bread that is eaten on Passover in commemoration of the haste in which the Israelites left Egypt.

MIKVAH: A pool of water deriving initially from a natural spring, rainwater, or melted natural ice. It is used in various ceremonies requiring ritual purification.

MINYAN: The minimum number of worshipers required for the recitation of prayers that may only be recited in the presence of a congregation. Traditionally the minyan is made up of ten males who have reached the age of Bar Mitzvah.

MITZVAH, MITZVOT (Heb. "commandment," "commandments"): One of traditional 613 divine injunctions found in the Torah. In colloquial use the term refers to any good deed.

MOHEL: Person who performs ritual circumcision.

NER TAMID: The Eternal Light commanded in the Torah as part of the furnishings of the Tabernacle in the Wilderness and later in the Temple in Jerusalem. It is recalled in most synagogues by a lamp that always remains lit.

ROSH HASHANAH: The Jewish New Year celebration commemorating the creation of the world. It ushers in a ten-day period of penitence culminating in Yom Kippur.

SEDER (Heb. "order"): The ritual meal that is served on the opening evenings of Passover in commemoration of the freeing of the Israelites from slavery in Egypt.

SIMCHA (Heb. "happiness"): A joyous occasion.

SHABBAS: The day of rest observed on the seventh day of the week in commemoration of God's rest upon completing the creation of the world and in memory of the fact that the Israelites were once slaves in Egypt.

SHAHARIT: The morning service recited daily after daybreak but before the first quarter of the day has passed.

SHUL: A Yiddish term for "synagogue."

TALMUD (Heb. "teaching"): A term used to designated the Mishnah (code of Jewish law promulgated by Judas ha-Nasi around the year 200) and the Gemara (the record of later rabbinic discussions about the Mishnah). Sometimes the term is used synonymously with Gemara.

TEFILLIN: Two small leather boxes bound to the arm and forehead by leather straps and containing four biblical passages (Exodus 13:1–10; Exodus 13:11–16; Deuteronomy 6:4–9; Deuteronomy 11:13–21).

TESHUVAH (Heb. "return"): Term used to indicate repentance, or return to God and the right way in which one should live.

TISHA B'AV: The ninth day of the month of Av is a day of fasting in commemoration of the destruction of the First and Second Temples.

TORAH (Heb. "teaching"): The term used to designate the first five books of the Bible (Genesis, Exodus, Leviticus, Numbers, and Deuteronomy). It is also used to refer to all of Jewish learning.

TREF (Heb. "torn"): Term used to designate all food, especially meat, that is not kosher.

TZEDAKAH: Term used to designate charitable contributions and behaviors.

YARMULKE: A Yiddish term for "skullcap."

YOM KIPPUR: The Day of Atonement, a day of fasting, reflecting on one's behavior, and praying for forgiveness.